W9-BDF-990

ENGINEERING MECHANICS
THIRD EDITION

STATICS STUDY PACK

FREE BODY DIAGRAM WORKBOOK
BY PETER SCHIAVONE
WORKING MODEL SIMULATION CD
BEDFORD AND FOWLER
PROBLEMS WEBSITE
BEDFORD AND FOWLER

BEDFORD   FOWLER

Prentice
Hall

PRENTICE HALL, Upper Saddle River, NJ 07458

Acquisitions Editor: Eric Svendsen
Managing Editor: David A. George
Production Editor: Blake Cooper
Supplement Cover Manager: Paul Gourhan
Supplement Cover Designer: PM Workshop Inc.
Manufacturing Buyer: Michael Bell

 © 2002 by Prentice-Hall, Inc.
Upper Saddle River, NJ 07458

All rights reserved. No part of this book may be
reproduced, in any form or by any means,
without permission in writing from the publisher.

Printed in the United States of America

10 9 8 7 6 5 4 3 2 1

ISBN   0-13-061574-9

Prentice-Hall International (UK) Limited, London
Prentice-Hall of Australia Pty. Limited, Sydney
Prentice-Hall Canada, Inc., Toronto
Prentice-Hall Hispanoamericana, S.A., Mexico City
Prentice-Hall of India Private Limited, New Delhi
Pearson Education Asia Pte. Ltd., Singapore
Prentice-Hall of Japan, Inc., Tokyo
Editora Prentice-Hall do Brazil, Ltda., Rio de Janeiro

Forward

The Statics Study Pack was designed to help students improve their study skills. It consists of three study components-a free body diagram workbook, a Visualization CD based on Working Model Software, and an access code to a website with over 500 sample Statics and Dynamics problems and solutions.

- Free Body Diagram Workbook – Prepared by Peter Schiavone of the University of Alberta. This workbook begins with a tutorial on free body diagrams and then includes 50 practice problems of progressing difficulty with complete solutions. Further "strategies and tips" help students understand how to use the diagrams in solving the accompanying problems.

- Working Model CD - This CD contains 25 pre-set simulations of Statics examples in the text that include questions for further exploration. Simulations are powered by the Working Model Engine and were created with actual artwork from the text to enhance their correlation with the text. Directions for CD installation are on the CD's README file. You need to have the CD in your drive when using the simulations. Please also note the licensing terms for using the CD. A set of questions associated with each simulation can be found in Appendix A of this workbook.

- Problems Website - Located at http://www.prenhall.com/bedford. This Website contains 500 sample Statics and Dynamics problems for students to study. Problems are keyed to each chapter of the text and contain complete solutions. All problems are supplemental and do not appear in the third edition. Student passwords are printed on the inside cover of the Free Body Diagram Workbook. To access this site, students should go to http://www.prenhall.com/bedford, choose the link for the Problems Website, and follow the on-line directions to register. This site also contains an unprotected section with multiple choice and True/False check up questions by Dr. Karim Nohra of the University of South Florida.

Preface

A thorough understanding of how to draw and use a free-body diagram
is absolutely essential when solving problems in mechanics.

This workbook consists mainly of a collection of problems intended to give the student practice in drawing and using free-body diagrams when solving problems in Statics.

All the problems are presented as tutorial problems with the solution only partially complete. The student is then expected to complete the solution by "filling in the blanks" in the spaces provided. This gives the student the opportunity to build free-body diagrams in stages and extract the relevant information from them when formulating equilibrium equations. Earlier problems provide students with partially drawn free-body diagrams and lots of hints to complete the solution. Later problems are more advanced and are designed to challenge the student more. The complete solution to each problem can be found at the back of the page. The problems are chosen from two-dimensional theories of particle and rigid body mechanics. Once the ideas and concepts developed in these problems have been understood and practiced, the student will find that they can be extended in a relatively straightforward manner to accommodate the corresponding three-dimensional theories.

The book begins with a brief primer on free-body diagrams: where they fit into the general procedure of solving problems in mechanics and why they are so important. Next follows a few examples to illustrate ideas and then the workbook problems.

For best results, the student should read the primer and then, beginning with the simpler problems, try to complete and understand the solution to each of the subsequent problems. The student should avoid the temptation to immediately look at the completed solution over the page. This solution should be accessed only as a last resort (after the student has struggled to the point of giving up), or to check the student's own solution after the fact. The idea behind this is very simple:

*We learn most when we **do** the thing we are trying to learn.*

In other words, reading through someone else's solution is not the same as actually working through the problem. In the former, the student gains *information*, in the latter the student gains *knowledge*. For example, how many people learn to swim or drive a car by reading an instruction manual?

Consequently, since this book is based on **doing**, the student who persistently solves the problems in this book will ultimately gain a thorough, usable knowledge of how to draw and use free-body diagrams.

P. Schiavone

Contents

1

Basic Concepts in Statics

Statics is a branch of mechanics that deals with the study of objects in *equilibrium*. In everyday conversation, equilibrium means an *unchanging state* or a *state of balance*. Examples of objects in equilibrium include pieces of furniture sitting at rest in a room or a person standing stationary on the sidewalk. If a train travels at constant speed on a straight track, objects that are at rest relative to the train, such as a person standing in the aisle, are in equilibrium since they are not accelerating. If the train should start to increase or decrease its speed, however, the person standing in the aisle would no longer be in equilibrium and might lose his balance.

More precisely, we say that objects are in equilibrium only if they are at rest (if originally at rest) or move with constant velocity (if originally in motion). The velocity must be measured relative to a frame of reference in which Newton's laws are valid, which is called an **inertial reference frame**. In most engineering applications, the velocity can be measured relative to the earth.

In mechanics, real objects (e.g. planets, cars, planes, tables, crates, etc) are represented or *modeled* using certain idealizations which simplify application of the relevant theory. In this book we refer to only two such models:

- **Particle or Point in Space.** A *particle* has mass but no size/shape. When an object's size/shape can be neglected so that only its mass is relevant to the description of its motion, the object can be modeled as a particle. This is the same thing as saying that the motion of the object can be modeled as the motion of a *point in space* (the point itself representing the center of mass of the moving object). For example, the size of an aircraft is insignificant when compared to the size of the earth and therefore the aircraft can be modeled as a particle (or point in space) when studying its three-dimensional motion in space.
- **Rigid Body.** A *rigid body* represents the next level of modeling sophistication after the particle. That is, a rigid body is a collection of particles (which therefore has mass) which has a significant size/shape but this size/shape cannot change. In other words, when an object is modeled as a rigid body, we assume that any deformations (changes in shape) are relatively small and can be neglected. Although any object does deform as it moves, if its deformation is small, *you can approximate its motion by modeling it as a rigid body*. For example, the actual deformations occurring in most structures and machines are relatively small so that the rigid body assumption is suitable in these cases.

1.1 Equilibrium

1.1.1 Equilibrium of an Object Modeled as a Particle

An object is in equilibrium provided it is at rest if originally at rest or has a constant velocity if originally in motion. To maintain equilibrium of an object modeled as a particle, it is necessary and sufficient to satisfy Newton's first law

1

of motion which requires the resultant force acting on the object (or, more precisely, the object's mass center) to be zero. In other words

$$\sum \mathbf{F} = \mathbf{0} \tag{1.1}$$

where $\sum \mathbf{F}$ is the vector sum of all the external forces acting on the object.

Successful application of the equilibrium equation (1.1) requires a complete specification of all the known and unknown external forces ($\sum \mathbf{F}$) that act on the object. The best way to account for these is to draw the object's *free-body diagram*.

1.1.2 Equilibrium of an Object Modeled as a Rigid Body

An object modeled as a particle is assumed to have no shape. Hence only external *forces* enter into the equilibrium equation (1.1).On the other hand, an object modeled as a rigid body is assumed to have mass *and* (unchanging) shape. Hence, both forces and moments need to be taken into account when writing down the corresponding equilibrium equations. In fact, an object modeled as a rigid body will be in equilibrium provided the sum of all the external forces acting on the object is equal to zero *and* the sum of the external moments taken about any point is equal to zero. In other words:

$$\sum \mathbf{F} = \mathbf{0} \tag{1.2}$$

$$\sum \mathbf{M}_O = \mathbf{0} \tag{1.3}$$

where $\sum \mathbf{F}$ is the vector sum of all the external forces acting on the rigid body and $\sum \mathbf{M}_O$ is the sum of the external moments about an arbitrary point O.

Successful application of the equations of equilibrium (1.2) and (1.3) requires a complete specification of all the known and unknown external forces ($\sum \mathbf{F}$) and moments ($\sum \mathbf{M}_O$) that act on the object. The best way to account for these is again to draw the object's *free-body diagram*.

2

Free-Body Diagrams: the Basics

2.1 Free-Body Diagram: Object Modeled as a Particle

The equilibrium equation (1.1) is used to determine unknown forces acting on an object (modeled as a particle) in equilibrium. The first step in doing this is to draw the *free-body diagram* of the object to identify the external forces acting on it. The object's free-body diagram is simply a sketch of the object *freed* from its surroundings showing *all* the (external) forces that *act* on it. The diagram focuses your attention on the object of interest and helps you identify *all* the external forces acting. For example:

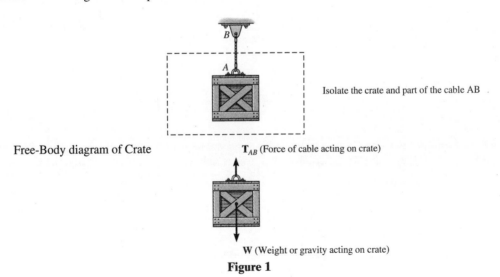

Isolate the crate and part of the cable AB

Free-Body diagram of Crate

$\mathbf{T}_{AB}$ (Force of cable acting on crate)

$\mathbf{W}$ (Weight or gravity acting on crate)

Figure 1

Note that once the crate is *separated* or *freed* from the system, forces which were previously internal to the system become external to the crate. For example, in Figure 1, such a force is the force of the cable AB *acting on the crate*.

Next, we present a formal procedure for drawing free-body diagrams for an object modeled as a particle.

2.1.1 Procedure for Drawing a Free-Body Diagram

1. *Identify the object you wish to isolate*. This choice is often dictated by the particular forces you wish to determine.

2. *Draw a sketch of the object isolated from its surroundings and show any relevant dimensions and angles.* Imagine the object to be isolated or cut free from the system of which it is a part. Your drawing should be reasonably accurate but it can omit irrelevant details.

3. *Show all external forces acting on the isolated object.* Indicate on this sketch *all* the external forces that act on the object. These forces can be *active forces*, which tend to set the object in motion, or they can be *reactive forces* which are the result of the constraints or supports that prevent motion. This stage is crucial: it may help to trace around the object's boundary, carefully noting each external force acting on it. Don't forget to include the weight of the object (unless it is being intentionally neglected).

4. *Identify and label each external force acting on the (isolated) object.* The forces that are known should be labeled with their known magnitudes and directions. Use letters to represent the magnitudes and arrows to represent the directions of forces that are unknown.

5. *The direction of a force having an unknown magnitude can be assumed.*

EXAMPLE 2.1

The crate in Figure 2 weighs 20lb. Draw free-body diagrams of the crate, the cord BD and the ring at B. Assume that the cords and the ring at B have negligible mass.

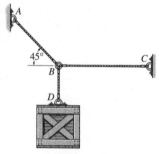

Figure 2

Solution

Free-Body Diagram for the Crate.   Imagine the crate to be isolated from its surroundings, then, by inspection, there are only two external forces acting on the crate, namely, the weight with magnitude 20lb and the force of the cord BD.

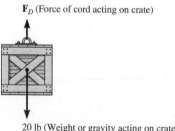

$\mathbf{F}_D$ (Force of cord acting on crate)

20 lb (Weight or gravity acting on crate)

Figure 3

Free-Body Diagram for the Cord BD**.**   Imagine the cord to be isolated from its surroundings, then, by inspection, there are only two external forces *acting on the cord*, namely, the force of the crate $\mathbf{F}_D$ and the force $\mathbf{F}_B$ caused by the ring. These forces both tend to pull on the cord so that the cord is in *tension*. Notice that $\mathbf{F}_D$ shown in this free-body diagram (Figure 4) is equal and opposite to that shown in Figure 3, a consequence of Newton's third law.

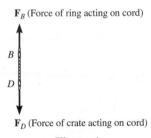

$\mathbf{F}_B$ (Force of ring acting on cord)

$\mathbf{F}_D$ (Force of crate acting on cord)

Figure 4

Free-Body Diagram for the ring at B   Imagine the ring to be isolated from its surroundings, then, by inspection, there are actually three external forces acting on the ring, all caused by the attached cords. Notice that $\mathbf{F}_B$ shown in this free-body diagram (Figure 5) is equal and opposite to that shown in Figure 4, a consequence of Newton's third law.   ◀

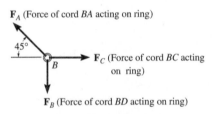

$\mathbf{F}_A$ (Force of cord BA acting on ring)

$\mathbf{F}_C$ (Force of cord BC acting on ring)

$\mathbf{F}_B$ (Force of cord BD acting on ring)

Figure 5

2.1.2 *Using the Free-Body Diagram: Solving Equilibrium Problems*

The free-body diagram is used to identify the unknown forces acting on the object when applying the equilibrium equation (1.1) to the object. The procedure for solving equilibrium problems is therefore as follows:

1. *Draw a free-body diagram*—you must choose an object to isolate that results in a free-body diagram including both known forces and forces you want to determine.
2. *Introduce a coordinate system* and establish the x, y-axes in any suitable orientation. Apply the equilibrium equation (1.1) in *component form* in each direction:

$$\sum F_x = 0 \text{ and } \sum F_y = 0 \qquad (2.1)$$

   to obtain equations relating the known and unknown forces.
3. Components are positive if they are directed along a positive axis and negative if they are directed along a negative axis.
4. If more than two unknowns exist and the problem involves a spring, apply $F = ks$ to relate the magnitude F of the spring force to the deformation s of the spring (here, k is the spring constant).
5. If the solution yields a negative result, this indicates the sense of the force is the reverse of that shown/assumed on the free-body diagram.

EXAMPLE 2.2

In Example 2.1, the free-body diagrams established in Figures 3–5 give us a picture of all the information we need to apply the equilibrium equations (2.1) to find the various unknown forces. In fact, taking the positive x-direction to be horizontal ($\rightarrow$ +) and the positive y-direction to be vertical ($\uparrow$ +), the equilibrium equations (2.1) when applied to each of the objects (regarded as particles) are:

For the Crate: $\uparrow + \sum F_y = 0$: $F_D - 20 = 0$ (See Figure 3)

$$F_D = 20 \text{ lb} \qquad (2.2)$$

For the Cord BD: $\uparrow + \sum F_y = 0$: $F_B - F_D = 0$ (See Figure 4)

$$F_B = F_D \qquad (2.3)$$

For the Ring: $\uparrow + \sum F_y = 0$: $F_A \sin 45° - F_B = 0$ (See Figure 5) (2.4)

$\rightarrow + \sum F_x = 0$: $F_C - F_A \cos 45° = 0$ (See Figure 5) (2.5)

Equations (2.2) - (2.5) are now 4 equations which can be solved for the 4 unknowns F_A, F_B, F_C and F_D. That is: $F_B = 20$ lb; $F_D = 20$ lb, $F_A = 28.28$ lb, $F_C = 20$ lb. These are the magnitudes of each of the forces $\mathbf{F_B}$, $\mathbf{F_D}$, $\mathbf{F_A}$ and $\mathbf{F_C}$, respectively. The corresponding directions of each of these forces is shown in the free-body diagrams above (Figures 3–5). ◄

2.2 Free-Body Diagram: Object Modeled as a Rigid Body

The equilibrium equations (1.2) and (1.3) are used to determine unknown forces and moments acting on an object (modeled as a rigid body) in equilibrium. The first step in doing this is again to draw the *free-body diagram* of the object to identify *all of* the external forces and moments acting on it. The procedure for drawing a free-body diagram in this case is much the same as that for an object modeled as a particle with the main exception that now, because the object's "size/shape" is taken into account, it can support also external couple moments and moments of external forces.

2.2.1 Procedure for Drawing a Free-Body Diagram: Rigid Body

1. Imagine the body to be isolated or "cut free" from its constraints and connections and sketch its outlined shape.
2. Identify all the external forces and couple moments that act on the body. Those generally encountered are:
   (a) Applied loadings
   (b) Reactions occurring at the supports or at points of contact with other bodies (See Table 2.1)
   (c) The weight of the body (applied at the body's center of gravity G)
3. The forces and couple moments that are known should be labeled with their proper magnitudes and directions. Letters are used to represent the magnitudes and direction angles of forces and couple moments that are *unknown*. Establish an x, y-coordinate system so that these unknowns, for example, A_x, B_y etc can be identified. Indicate the dimensions of the body necessary for computing the moments of external forces. In particular, if a force or couple moment has a known line of action but unknown magnitude, the arrowhead which defines the sense of the vector can be assumed. The correctness of the assumed sense will become apparent after solving the equilibrium equations for the unknown magnitude. By definition, the magnitude of a vector is *always positive*, so that if the solution yields a *negative* scalar, the *minus sign* indicates that the vector's sense is *opposite* to that which was originally assumed.

Table 2.1. Supports used in Two-Dimensional Applications

Supports	Reactions
Rope or Cable Spring	One Collinear Force
Contact with a Smooth Surface	One Force Normal to the Supporting Surface
Contact with a Rough Surface	Two Force Components
Pin Support	Two Force Components
Roller Support Equivalents	One Force Normal to the Supporting Surface
Constrained Pin or Slider	One Normal Force
Built-in (Fixed) Support	Two Force Components and One Couple

Important Points

- No equilibrium problem should be solved without first drawing the free-body diagram, so as to account for all the external forces and moments that act on the body.

- If a support *prevents translation* of a body in a particular direction, then the support exerts a force on the body to prevent translation in that direction.

- If *rotation is prevented* then the support exerts a couple moment on the body.

- Internal forces are never shown on the free-body diagram since they occur in equal but opposite collinear pairs and therefore cancel each other out.

- The weight of a body is an external force and its effect is shown as a single resultant force acting through the body's center of gravity G.

- *Couple moments* can be placed anywhere on the free-body diagram since they are *free vectors*. Forces can act at any point along their lines of action since they are *sliding vectors*.

EXAMPLE 2.3

Draw the free-body diagram of the beam of mass 10 kg. The beam is pin-connected at A and rocker-supported at B.

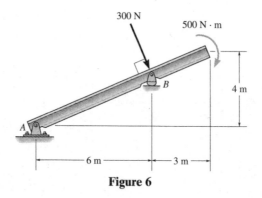

Figure 6

Solution

The free-body diagram of the beam is shown in Figure 7. From Table 2.1, since the support at A is a pin-connection, there are two reactions acting *on the beam at* A denoted by $\mathbf{A}_x$ and $\mathbf{A}_y$. In addition, there is one reaction *acting on the beam* at the rocker support at B. We denote this reaction by the force $\mathbf{F}$ which acts perpendicular to the surface at B, the point of contact (see Table 2.1). The magnitudes of these vectors are *unknown* and their sense has been *assumed* (the correctness of the assumed sense will become apparent after solving the equilibrium equations for the unknown magnitude i.e. if application of the equilibrium equations to the beam yields a negative result for the magnitude F, this indicates the sense of the force is the reverse of that shown/assumed on the free-body diagram). The weight of the beam acts through the beam's mass center. ◄

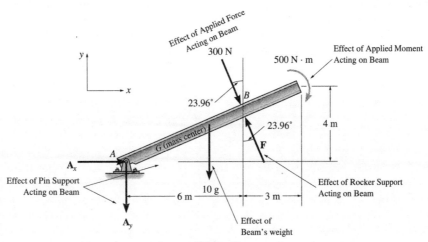

Figure 7

2.2.2 Using the Free-Body Diagram: Equilibrium

The equilibrium equations (1.2) and (1.3) can be written in component form as:

$$\sum F_x = 0, \tag{2.6}$$

$$\sum F_y = 0, \tag{2.7}$$

$$\sum M_O = 0, \tag{2.8}$$

Here, $\sum F_x$ and $\sum F_y$ represent, respectively, the algebraic sums of the x and y components of all the external forces acting on the body and $\sum M_O$ represents the algebraic sum of the couple moments and the moments of all the external force components about an axis perpendicular to the x–y plane and passing through the arbitrary point O, which may lie either on or off the body. The procedure for solving equilibrium problems for a rigid body once the free-body diagram for the body is established, is as follows:

- Apply the moment equation of equilibrium (2.8), about a point (O) that lies at the intersection of the lines of action of two unknown forces. In this way, the moments of these unknowns are zero about O and a direct solution for the third unknown can be determined.

- When applying the force equilibrium equations (2.6) and (2.7), orient the x and y-axes along lines that will provide the simplest resolution of the forces into their x and y components.

- If the solution of the equilibrium equations yields a negative scalar for a force or couple moment magnitude, this indicates that the sense is opposite to that which was assumed on the free-body diagram.

EXAMPLE 2.4

The pipe assembly has a built-in support and is subjected to two forces and a couple moment as shown. Find the reactions at A.

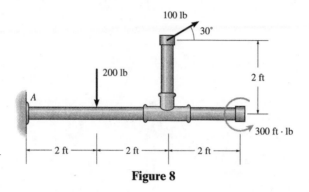

Figure 8

Solution

Free-Body Diagram   The first thing to do is to draw the free-body diagram of the assembly in order to identify all the external forces and moments acting. We isolate the assembly from its built-in support at A (that way the reactions at A become external forces acting on the assembly). There are three unknown reactions at A: two force components A_x and A_y and a couple M_A (see Table 2.1). It might also be useful to resolve the applied 100 lb force into its components in anticipation of the application of the equilibrium equations (2.6)–(2.8).   ◄

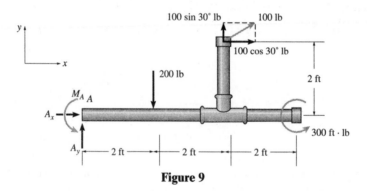

Figure 9

Equilibrium Equations   The free-body diagram of the assembly suggests we can sum moments about the point A to eliminate the moment contribution of the reaction forces $\mathbf{A}_x$ and $\mathbf{A}_y$ acting on the beam. The equilibrium equations (2.6)–(2.8) are then:

$$\rightarrow +\sum F_x = 0 : \quad A_x + 100\cos 30° = 0$$
$$\uparrow +\sum F_y = 0 : \quad A_y - 200 + 100\sin 30° = 0$$

Taking counterclockwise as positive when computing moments, we have:

$$\sum M_A = 0 : \quad M_A + 300 - (200)(2) - (100\cos 30°)(2) + (100\sin 30°)(4) = 0$$

(Notice that since the moment due to a couple is the same about any point, the moment about point A due to the 300 ft-lb counterclockwise couple is 300 ft-lb counterclockwise.) Solving these three equations we obtain the reaction components:

$$\boxed{A_x = -86.6 \text{ lb}, \qquad A_y = 150.0 \text{ lb.}}$$

(Note that we have obtained a negative value for A_x which means that the sense or direction of the force $\mathbf{A}_x$ is opposite to that which was assumed on the free-body diagram.

3

Problems

3.1 Free-Body Diagrams in Particle Equilibrium

In each of the following problems, assume that the objects are in equilibrium.

Problem 3.1.

The cables are used to support a block having a weight of 1000 lb. Draw a free-body diagram for the ring at A. The weight of the ring is negligible.

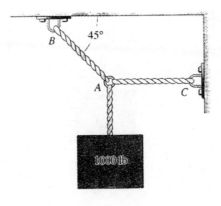

Solution

1. The ring acts only as a cable juncture and hence can be modeled as a particle (whose weight we are told to neglect).

2. Imagine the ring at A to be separated or detached from the system.

3. The (detached) ring at A is subjected to three *external* forces. They are caused by (remember to neglect the weight of the ring):

   i.   **ii.**

   iii.

4. Draw the free-body diagram of the (detached) ring showing all these forces labeled with their magnitudes and directions. You should also include any other available information e.g. lengths, angles etc—which will help when formulating the equilibrium equations for the pulley.

Problem 3.1.

The cables are used to support a block having a weight of 1000 lb. Draw a free-body diagram for the ring at A. The weight of the ring is negligible.

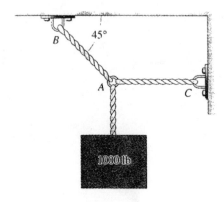

Solution

1. The ring acts only as a cable juncture and hence can be modeled as a particle (whose weight we are told to neglect).
2. Imagine the ring at A to be separated or detached from the system.
3. The (detached) ring at A is subjected to three *external* forces. They are caused by (remember to neglect the weight of the ring):

   i. **CABLE** AB ii. **CABLE** AC

   iii. The 1000 lb **WEIGHT**
4. Draw the free-body diagram of the (detached) ring showing all these forces labeled with their magnitudes and directions. You should also include any other available information e.g. lengths, angles etc—which will help when formulating the equilibrium equations for the pulley.

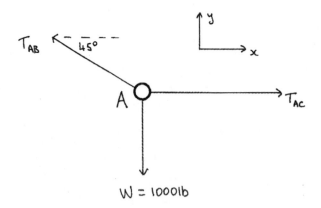

T_{AB}: Magnitude of force from cable AB on ring.

T_{AC}: Magnitude of force from cable AC on ring.

W: Weight of block on ring.

Problem 3.2.

The 200 lb horizontal bar is suspended by the springs A, B and C. The unstretched lengths of the springs are equal. The spring constants are k_A, k_B and k_C, respectively, with $k_A = k_C$. Draw a free-body diagram of the bar.

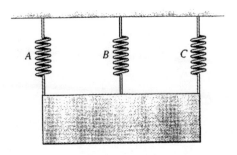

Solution

1. Imagine the bar to be separated or detached from the system.
2. The (detached) bar is subjected to four *external* forces. They are caused by:

   i.   **ii.**

   iii.   **iv.**

3. Draw the free-body diagram of the (detached) bar showing all these forces labeled with their magnitudes and directions. You should also include any other available information e.g. lengths, angles etc—which will help when formulating the equilibrium equations for the bar.

Problem 3.2.

The 200 lb horizontal bar is suspended by the springs A, B and C. The unstretched lengths of the springs are equal. The spring constants are k_A, k_B and k_C, respectively, with $k_A = k_C$. Draw a free-body diagram of the bar.

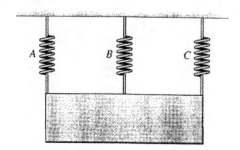

Solution

1. Imagine the bar to be separated or detached from the system.

2. The (detached) bar is subjected to four *external* forces. They are caused by:

    i. **SPRING** A ii. **SPRING** B

    iii. **SPRING** C iv. **THE BAR'S WEIGHT** (200 lb)

3. Draw the free-body diagram of the (detached) bar showing all these forces labeled with their magnitudes and directions. You should also include any other available information e.g. lengths, angles etc—which will help when formulating the equilibrium equations for the bar.

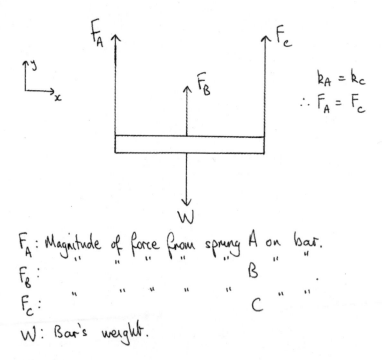

F_A: Magnitude of force from spring A on bar.

F_B: " " " " " B " "

F_C: " " " " " C " "

W: Bar's weight.

Problem 3.3.

The system of frictionless pulleys is in equilibrium. Draw separate free-body diagrams of the pulley at A and the bar at B. Neglect the weight of the pulleys.

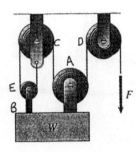

Solution

1. Imagine the pulley at A and the bar at B to be separated or detached from the system.
2. The (detached) pulley at A is subjected to three *external* forces.
   They are caused by (remember that a frictionless pulley changes the direction of a force but not its magnitude):

   i.   **ii.**

   iii.

   The (detached) bar at B is subjected to three *external* forces. They are caused by:

   i.   **ii.**

   iii.

3. Draw the free-body diagram of the (detached) pulley and the detached bar showing all these forces labeled with their magnitudes and directions. You should also include any other available information e.g. lengths, angles etc - which will help when formulating the equilibrium equations.

Problem 3.3.

The system of frictionless pulleys is in equilibrium. Draw separate free-body diagrams of the pulley at A and the bar at B. Neglect the weight of the pulleys.

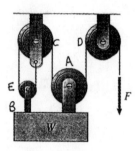

Solution

1. Imagine the pulley at A and the bar at B to be separated or detached from the system.
2. The (detached) pulley at A is subjected to three *external* forces. They are caused by (remember that a frictionless pulley changes the direction of a force but not its magnitude):

   i. CORD AC **ii. CORD** AD

   iii. REACTION OF WEIGHT ON PULLEY A

   The (detached) bar at B is subjected to three *external* forces. They are caused by:

   i. REACTION OF PULLEY A **ON WEIGHT**   **ii. REACTION OF PULLEY** E **ON WEIGHT**

   iii. THE WEIGHT W

3. Draw the free-body diagram of the (detached) pulley and the detached bar showing all these forces labeled with their magnitudes and directions. You should also include any other available information e.g. lengths, angles etc - which will help when formulating the equilibrium equations.

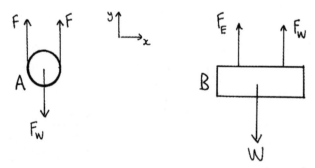

F_W: Magnitude of reaction of bar on pulley A.

F_E: Magnitude of reaction of pulley E on bar.

NOTE: For equilibrium, $F_W = 2F$, $F_E = F_W$.

Problem 3.4.

The rocket is suspended by two cables. The mass of the rocket is 45 Mg. Draw a free-body diagram of the support collar at A.

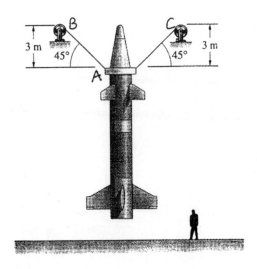

Solution

1. Imagine the collar at A to be separated or detached from the system.
2. The (detached) collar is subjected to three *external* forces. They are caused by:

   i.   ii.

   iii.

3. Draw the free-body diagram of the (detached) collar showing all these forces labeled with their magnitudes and directions. You should also include any other available information e.g. lengths, angles etc—which will help when formulating the equilibrium equations for the pulley.

Problem 3.4.

The rocket is suspended by two cables. The mass of the rocket is 45Mg. Draw a free-body diagram of the support collar at *A*.

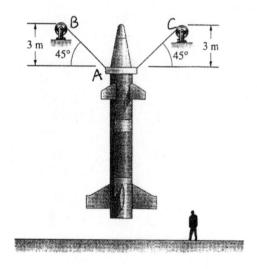

Solution

1. Imagine the collar at *A* to be separated or detached from the system.
2. The (detached) collar is subjected to three *external* forces. They are caused by:

   i. CABLE *AB*   **ii. CABLE** *AC*

   iii. WEIGHT OF COLLAR

3. Draw the free-body diagram of the (detached) collar showing all these forces labeled with their magnitudes and directions. You should also include any other available information e.g. lengths, angles etc—which will help when formulating the equilibrium equations for the pulley.

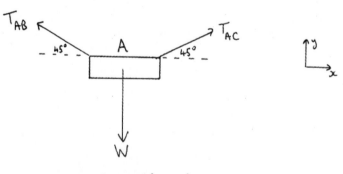

T_{AB} : Magnitude of force from cable AB on collar.

T_{AC} :   "   "   "   "   "   AC   "   "

W : Weight on collar.

Problem 3.5.

A construction worker holds a 500-lb crate in the (equilibrium) position shown. Draw a free-body diagram for the cable juncture at A. Neglect the mass of the cable juncture.

Solution

1. Imagine the cable juncture to be separated or detached from the system.

2. The (detached) cable juncture is subjected to three *external* forces. They are caused by:

   i.   **ii.**

   iii.

3. Draw the free-body diagram of the (detached) juncture showing all these forces labeled with their magnitudes and directions. You should also include any other available information e.g. lengths, angles etc—which will help when formulating the equilibrium equations.

O^A

Problem 3.5.

A construction worker holds a 500-lb crate in the (equilibrium) position shown. Draw a free-body diagram for the cable juncture at A. Neglect the mass of the cable juncture.

Solution

1. Imagine the cable juncture to be separated or detached from the system.

2. The (detached) cable juncture is subjected to three *external* forces. They are caused by:

   i. TENSION IN CABLE AB **ii. FORCE EXERTED BY WORKER THROUGH CABLE** AC

   iii. WEIGHT OF CRATE

3. Draw the free-body diagram of the (detached) juncture showing all these forces labeled with their magnitudes and directions. You should also include any other available information e.g. lengths, angles etc—which will help when formulating the equilibrium equations.

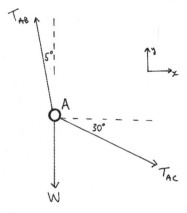

T_{AB}: Magnitude of force in cable AB on cable juncture A.

T_{AC}: " " " " AC " " " "

W: Weight of crate on cable juncture A.

Problem 3.6.

The steel ball has a weight of 100 lb and is being hoisted at uniform velocity. The system is held in equilibrium at angle θ by the appropriate force in each cord. Draw the free-body diagram for the *small* pulley.

Solution

1. The pulley has *negligible shape* (we are told it is *small*) so that it can be modeled as a particle.
2. Imagine the pulley to be separated or detached from the system.
3. The (detached) pulley is subjected to three *external* forces. They are caused by:

   i.   **ii.**

   iii.

4. Draw the free-body diagram of the (detached) pulley showing all these forces labeled with their magnitudes and directions. You should also include any other available information e.g. lengths, angles etc—which will help when formulating the equilibrium equations for the pulley.

O

Problem 3.6.

The steel ball has a weight of 100 lb and is being hoisted at uniform velocity. The system is held in equilibrium at angle θ by the appropriate force in each cord. Draw the free-body diagram for the *small* pulley.

Solution

1. The pulley has *negligible shape* (we are told it is *small*) so that it can be modeled as a particle.
2. Imagine the pulley to be separated or detached from the system.
3. The (detached) pulley is subjected to three *external* forces. They are caused by:

      i. CORD AB **ii. FORCE T**

      iii. WEIGHT OF BALL

4. Draw the free-body diagram of the (detached) pulley showing all these forces labeled with their magnitudes and directions. You should also include any other available information e.g. lengths, angles etc—which will help when formulating the equilibrium equations for the pulley.

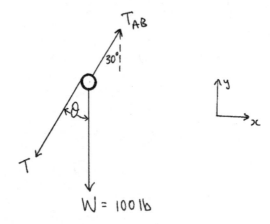

T: Magnitude of force T on pulley.

T_{AB}: Magnitude of force in cord AB on pulley.

W: Weight of ball on pulley.

Problem 3.7.

The system is in equilibrium. Draw free-body diagrams for the block *A* and disk *B*.

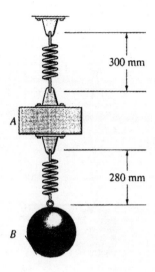

Solution

1. Imagine the block and the disk to be separated or detached from the system.
2. Block *A* is subjected to three *external* forces. They are caused by:

   i.   **ii.**

   iii.

   Disk *B* is subjected to two external forces caused by:

   i.   **ii.**

3. Draw the free-body diagrams of block *A* and disk *B* showing all these forces labeled with their magnitudes and directions.

Problem 3.7.

The system is in equilibrium. Draw free-body diagrams for the block A and disk B.

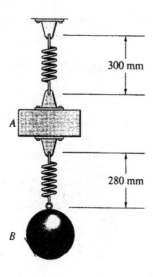

300 mm

280 mm

Solution

1. Imagine the block and the disk to be separated or detached from the system.
2. Block A is subjected to three *external* forces. They are caused by:

      i. TENSION IN UPPER SPRING   **ii. TENSION IN LOWER SPRING**

      iii. WEIGHT OF BLOCK A

   Disk B is subjected to two external forces caused by:

      i. TENSION IN LOWER SPRING   **ii. WEIGHT OF DISK** B

3. Draw the free-body diagrams of block A and disk B showing all these forces labeled with their magnitudes and directions.

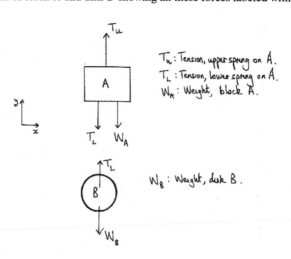

T_u : Tension, upper spring on A.
T_L : Tension, lower spring on A.
W_A : Weight, block A.

W_B : Weight, disk B.

Problem 3.8.

The 50-kg load is supported at A by a system of five cords. Draw the free-body diagrams for the rings at A and B when the system is in equilibrium.

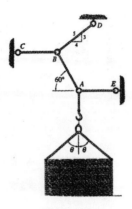

Solution

1. Imagine A and B to be separated or detached from the system.

2. Each of A and B is subjected to three *external* forces. For A, they are caused by:

   i.   **ii.**

   iii.

For B, they are caused by:

   i.   **ii.**

   iii.

3. Draw the free-body diagrams of A and B showing all these forces labeled with their magnitudes and directions. You should also include any other available information e.g. lengths, angles etc—which will help when formulating the equilibrium equations.

Problem 3.8.

The 50-kg load is supported at A by a system of five cords. Draw the free-body diagrams for the rings at A and B when the system is in equilibrium.

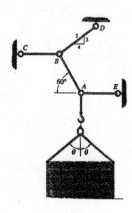

Solution

1. Imagine A and B to be separated or detached from the system.
2. Each of A and B is subjected to three *external* forces. For A, they are caused by:
   - **i. CABLE** AB
   - **ii. CABLE** AE
   - **iii. WEIGHT OF LOAD**

   For B, they are caused by:
   - **i. CABLE** BC
   - **ii. CABLE** BD
   - **iii. CABLE** BA

3. Draw the free-body diagrams of A and B showing all these forces labeled with their magnitudes and directions. You should also include any other available information e.g. lengths, angles etc—which will help when formulating the equilibrium equations.

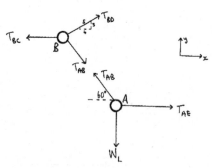

T_{AB} : Magnitude of force in cable AB on A.
T_{AE} :   "   "   "   "   " AE "   "
T_{BD} :   "   "   "   "   " BD on B.
T_{BC} :   "   "   "   "   " BC on B
W_L : Weight of load on A.

Problem 3.9.

The system is in equilibrium. Draw free-body diagrams for each pulley and the suspended object A.

Solution

1. Imagine each pulley and the object to be separated or detached from the system.
2. Each (detached) pulley and the object at A is subjected to four *external* forces, *not* all independent.
3. Draw free-body diagrams of each (detached) pulley and the object showing all these forces labeled with their magnitudes and directions.

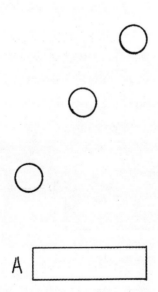

A

Problem 3.9.

The system is in equilibrium. Draw free-body diagrams for each pulley and the suspended object A.

Solution

1. Imagine each pulley and the object to be separated or detached from the system.
2. Each (detached) pulley and the object at A is subjected to four *external* forces, *not* all independent.
3. Draw free-body diagrams of each (detached) pulley and the object showing all these forces labeled with their magnitudes and directions.

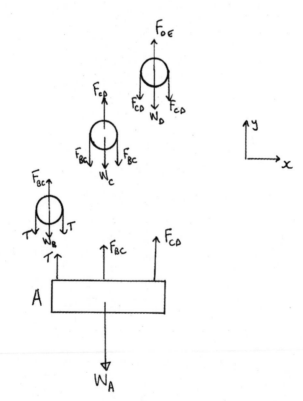

Problem 3.10.

The airplane is in steady flight. Draw a free-body diagram of the airplane and use it to write down the equilibrium equations for the airplane.

Solution

1. Imagine the airplane to be separated or detached from the system (airplane + sky).
2. The (detached) airplane is subjected to four *external* forces. They are caused by:

   i.   ii.

   iii.   iv.

3. Draw the free-body diagram of the (detached) airplane showing all these forces labeled with their magnitudes and directions. Include any other relevant information e.g. lengths, angles etc

4. Establish an xy-axes system on the free-body diagram and write down the equilibrium equations in each of the x and $y-$ directions. Take the $x - axis$ to be along the path of the airplane.

   $+\nwarrow \sum F_x = 0:$

   $+\nearrow \sum F_y = 0:$

Problem 3.10.

The airplane is in steady flight. Draw a free-body diagram of the airplane and use it to write down the equilibrium equations for the airplane.

Solution

1. Imagine the airplane to be separated or detached from the system (airplane + sky).
2. The (detached) airplane is subjected to four *external* forces. They are caused by:

   i. DRAG D **ii. LIFT** L

   iii. THRUST T **iv. WEIGHT** W

3. Draw the free-body diagram of the (detached) airplane showing all these forces labeled with their magnitudes and directions. Include any other relevant information e.g. lengths, angles etc

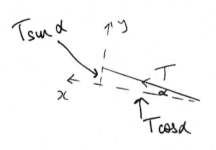
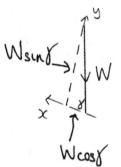

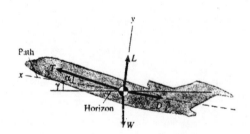

4. Establish an xy-axes system on the free-body diagram and write down the equilibrium equations in each of the x and $y-$ directions. Take the $x - axis$ to be along the path of the airplane.

$$+\nwarrow \sum F_x = 0: \quad T\cos\alpha - D - W\sin\gamma = 0$$

$$+\nearrow \sum F_y = 0: \quad T\sin\alpha + L - W\cos\gamma = 0$$

Problem 3.11.

The cord suspends the *small* bucket in the equilibrium position shown. The spring has an unstretched length of 3—ft and the system is in equilibrium at angle θ. Draw the free-body diagram of the connecting knot at A and write down the equilibrium equations for the knot at A.

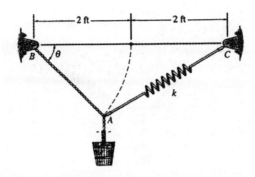

Solution

1. The knot at A has *negligible shape* so that it can be modelled as a particle.
2. Imagine the knot at A to be separated or detached from the system.
3. The (detached) knot at A is subjected to three *external* forces. They are caused by:

   i.   **ii.**

   iii.

4. Draw the free-body diagram of the (detached) knot showing all these forces labeled with their magnitudes and directions.

5. Establish an xy-axes system on the free-body diagram and write down the equilibrium equations in each of the x and $y-$ directions

$$+\rightarrow \sum F_x = 0:$$

$$+\uparrow \ \ \sum F_y = 0:$$

Problem 3.11.

The cord suspends the *small* bucket in the equilibrium position shown. The spring has an unstretched length of 3—ft and the system is in equilibrium at angle θ. Draw the free-body diagram of the connecting knot at A and write down the equilibrium equations for the knot at A.

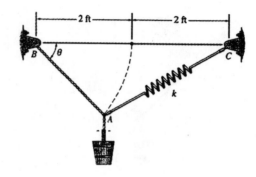

Solution

1. The knot at A has *negligible shape* so that it can be modelled as a particle.
2. Imagine the knot at A to be separated or detached from the system.
3. The (detached) knot at A is subjected to three *external* forces. They are caused by:

   i. CORD AB **ii. SPRING** AC

   iii. WEIGHT OF BUCKET

4. Draw the free-body diagram of the (detached) knot showing all these forces labeled with their magnitudes and directions.

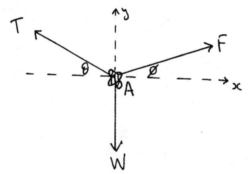

T: Magnitude of force of cord AB on A.

F_s: "   "   "   " spring AC on A.

W: Weight of bucket on A.

5. Establish an xy-axes system on the free-body diagram and write down the equilibrium equations in each of the x and $y-$ directions

   $+\rightarrow \sum F_x = 0:$ $F_s \cos \phi - T \cos \theta = 0.$

   $+\uparrow \;\; \sum F_y = 0:$ $T \sin \theta + F_s \sin \phi - W = 0.$

Problem 3.12.

The mass of the cylinder A is 30 kg. Draw separate free-body diagrams for the cylinder A and the pulley B. Use these free-body diagrams to formulate equilibrium equations for both the cylinder and the pulley. Use these equilibrium equations to find the mass of the pulley B.

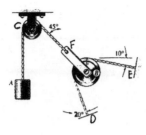

Solution

1. Imagine the cylinder A to be separated or detached from the system.
2. The (detached) cylinder is subjected to two *external* forces. They are caused by:

   i.   **ii.**

3. Imagine the pulley B to be separated or detached from the system.
4. The (detached) pulley is subjected to four *external* forces.
        They are caused by:

   i.   **ii.**

   iii.   **iv.**

   (Note that the tensions in both sides of the cord going around pulley B have the same magnitude)
5. Draw the free-body diagram of the (detached) pulley showing these forces labeled with their magnitudes and directions.

A ▯   Ⓑ

6. Establish an xy-axes system on each free-body diagram and write down the equilibrium equations for each of the cylinder A and the pulley B :

   Cylinder:
   $+\uparrow \ \sum F_y = 0 :$
   Pulley:
   $+\rightarrow \ \sum F_x = 0 :$

   $+\uparrow \ \sum F_y = 0 :$

   You should have obtained three equations for three unknowns (the tensions in both sides of the cord going around pulley B have the same magnitude), one of which is m_{pulley} , the required mass of the pulley B. Solve these equations to obtain m_{pulley}.

Problem 3.12.

The mass of the cylinder A is 30 kg. Draw separate free-body diagrams for the cylinder A and the pulley B. Use these free-body diagrams to formulate equilibrium equations for both the cylinder and the pulley. Use these equilibrium equations to find the mass of the pulley B.

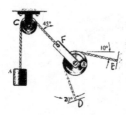

Solution

1. Imagine the cylinder A to be separated or detached from the system.
2. The (detached) cylinder is subjected to two *external* forces. They are caused by:

   i. TENSION IN CORD AC **ii. WEIGHT OF CYLINDER** A

3. Imagine the pulley B to be separated or detached from the system.
4. The (detached) pulley is subjected to four *external* forces. They are caused by:

   i. PULLEY'S WEIGHT   **ii. TENSION IN CORD** BD

   iii. TENSION IN CORD BE **iv. FORCE ON PULLEY FROM** BF

   (Note that the tensions in both sides of the cord going around pulley B have the same magnitude)

5. Draw the free-body diagram of the (detached) pulley showing these forces labeled with their magnitudes and directions.

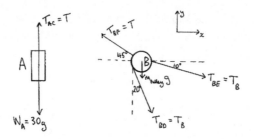

6. Establish an xy-axes system on each free-body diagram and write down the equilibrium equations for each of the cylinder A and the pulley B :

   Cylinder:

   $+\uparrow \ \sum F_y = 0 : \quad T - 30g = 0$

   Pulley:

   $+\rightarrow \ \sum F_x = 0 : \quad -T \cos 45° + T_B \cos 10° + T_B \sin 20° = 0$

   $+\uparrow \ \sum F_y = 0 : \quad T \sin 45° - T_B \sin 10° - T_B \cos 20° - m_{pulley}g = 0$ (Here, $T_B = T_{BE} = T_{BD}$ (frictionless pulley))

   You should have obtained three equations in three unknowns, one of which is m_{pulley}, the required mass of the pulley B. Solve these equations to obtain m_{pulley} :

   $T = 294.3N$

   $T_B = T_{BE} = T_{BD} = 156.8N$

   $m_{pulley} = 3.41kg$

Problem 3.13.

The post anchors a cable that helps support an oil derrick. If $\alpha = 35°$ and $\beta = 50°$, draw a free-body diagram for the ring (cable juncture) at A. Use this free-body diagram to formulate appropriate equilibrium equations. Use these equations to find the tensions in cables AB and AC in terms of the tension T.

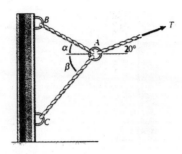

Solution

1. Imagine the ring at A to be separated or detached from the system.
2. The (detached) ring at A is subjected to three *external* forces. They are caused by:

   i.   **ii.**

   iii.

3. Draw the free-body diagram of the (detached) ring showing all these forces labeled with their magnitudes and directions. Include also any other information which may help when formulating the equilibrium equations for the ring.

A

4. Establish an xy-axes system on the free-body diagram and write down the equilibrium equations in the x and $y-$ directions:

   $$+\rightarrow \sum F_x = 0$$

   $$+\uparrow \;\; \sum F_y = 0 :$$

5. Solve for the required tensions in terms of the tension T:

Problem 3.13.

The post anchors a cable that helps support an oil derrick. If $\alpha = 35°$ and $\beta = 50°$, draw a free-body diagram for the ring (cable juncture) at A. Use this free-body diagram to formulate appropriate equilibrium equations. Use these equations to find the tensions in cables AB and AC in terms of the tension T.

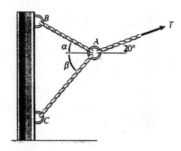

Solution

1. Imagine the ring at A to be separated or detached from the system.
2. The (detached) ring at A is subjected to three *external* forces. They are caused by:

   i. CABLE AB **ii. CABLE** AC

   iii. FORCE OF MAGNITUDE T

3. Draw the free-body diagram of the (detached) ring showing all these forces labeled with their magnitudes and directions. Include also any other information which may help when formulating the equilibrium equations for the ring.

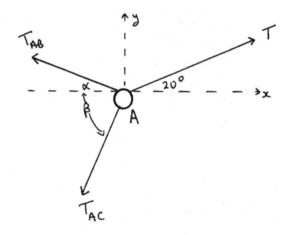

4. Establish an xy-axes system on the free-body diagram and write down the equilibrium equations in the x and $y-$ directions:

$$+\rightarrow \ \sum F_x = 0: \quad T\cos 20° - T_{AB}\cos\alpha - T_{AC}\cos\beta = 0$$
$$+\uparrow \ \sum F_y = 0: \quad T\sin 20° + T_{AB}\sin\alpha - T_{AC}\sin\beta = 0$$

5. Solve for the required tensions in terms of the tension T, noting that $\alpha = 35°$ and $\beta = 50°$:

$$T_{AC} = \frac{\sin(\alpha + 20°)}{\sin(\alpha + \beta)}T = 0.8223T$$

$$T_{AB} = \frac{\sin(\beta - 20°)}{\sin(\alpha + \beta)}T = 0.5019T$$

Problem 3.14.

The following system lies on the surface of the planet Mars (acceleration due to gravity $= 4.02 m/s^2 \downarrow$). The unstretched length of the spring AB is 660 mm and the spring constant $k = 1000$ N/m. draw a free-body diagram of the connector at A and use it to find the mass of the object suspended from A.

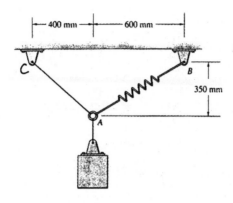

Solution

1. Imagine the connector to be separated or detached from the system.
2. The (detached) connector is subjected to three *external* forces. They are caused by:

   i.   **ii.**

   iii.

3. Draw the free-body diagram of the (detached) connector showing all these forces labeled with their magnitudes and directions. Include any other relevant information e.g. lengths, angles etc

4. Establish an xy-axes system on the free-body diagram and write down the equilibrium equations in each of the x and $y-$ directions

   $+\rightarrow \sum F_x = 0 :$

   $+\uparrow \sum F_y = 0 :$

5. Find the extension of and hence the magnitude of the tension in the spring AB using the linear spring force-extension relation:

6. Solve the above three equations for three unknowns including the weight of the suspended object:

7. Find the mass of the suspended object:

Problem 3.14.

The following system lies on the surface of the planet Mars (acceleration due to gravity $= 4.02 m/s^2 \downarrow$). The unstretched length of the spring AB is 660 mm and the spring constant $k = 1000$ N/m. Draw a free-body diagram of the connector at A and use it to find the mass of the object suspended from A.

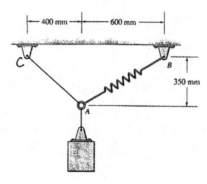

Solution

1. Imagine the connector to be separated or detached from the system.

2. The (detached) connector is subjected to three *external* forces. They are caused by:

   i. CABLE AC **ii. SPRING** AB

   iii. WEIGHT OF OBJECT AT A

3. Draw the free-body diagram of the (detached) connector showing all these forces labeled with their magnitudes and directions. Include any other relevant information e.g. lengths, angles etc

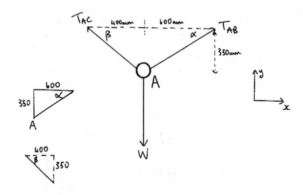

4. Establish an xy-axes system on the free-body diagram and write down the equilibrium equations in each of the x and $y-$ directions

$$+\rightarrow \; \Sigma F_x = 0: \quad T_{AB} \cos\alpha - T_{AC} \cos\beta = 0 \tag{1}$$

$$+\uparrow \;\; \Sigma F_y = 0: \quad T_{AC} \sin\alpha - T_{AB} \sin\beta - W = 0 \tag{2}$$

5. Find the extension of and hence the magnitude of the tension in the spring AB using the linear spring force-extension relation: Spring extension is: $\Delta L = \sqrt{(350)^2 + (600)^2} - 660 = 34.62 mm$ $T_{AB} = k\Delta L = (1000)(0.03462) = 34.6N$ (3)

6. Solve the above three equations for three unknowns including the weight of the suspended object: Noting that $\tan\alpha = \frac{350}{600}$, $\tan\beta = \frac{350}{400}$, we obtain: $\alpha = 30.26°$, $\beta = 41.1°$ Solving the three equations (1) - (3) leads to: $W = 43.62N$

7. Find the mass of the suspended object: $m = \frac{W}{g} = \frac{43.62}{4.02} = 10.85 kg$.

Problem 3.15.

The breeches buoy is used to transfer the person B between two ships. The person is attached to a pulley that rolls on the overhead cable. The total weight of the person and the buoy is 250 lb. Draw a free-body diagram of the person at B and use it to find the tension in the horizontal line AB necessary to hold the person in equilibrium in the position shown.

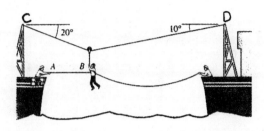

Solution

1. The person at B has *negligible shape* and so can be modelled as a particle.
2. Imagine the person to be separated or detached from the system.
3. The (detached) person is subjected to four *external* forces. They are caused by:

   i.   **ii.**

   iii.   **iv.**

4. Draw the free-body diagram of the (detached) person showing all these forces labeled with their magnitudes and directions. Include any other relevant information e.g. lengths, angles etc

5. Establish an xy-axes system on the free-body diagram and write down the equilibrium equations in each of the x and $y-$ directions

$$+\rightarrow \sum F_x = 0:$$

$$+\uparrow \sum F_y = 0:$$

6. Solve these equations to find the required tension in the line AB:

Problem 3.15.

The breeches buoy is used to transfer the person B between two ships. The person is attached to a pulley that rolls on the overhead cable. The total weight of the person and the buoy is 250 lb. Draw a free-body diagram of the person at B and use it to find the tension in the horizontal line AB necessary to hold the person in equilibrium in the position shown.

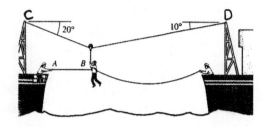

Solution

1. The person at B has *negligible shape* and so can be modelled as a particle.
2. Imagine the person to be separated or detached from the system.
3. The (detached) person is subjected to four *external* forces. They are caused by:

   i. **CABLE** BC ii. **CABLE** BD

   iii. **CABLE** BA iv. **TOTAL WEIGHT OF PERSON AND BUOY**
                                                  ($W = 250$ lb)

4. Draw the free-body diagram of the (detached) person showing all these forces labeled with their magnitudes and directions. Include any other relevant information e.g. lengths, angles etc

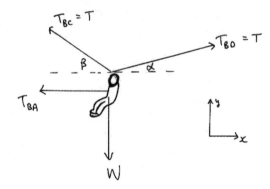

5. Establish an xy-axes system on the free-body diagram and write down the equilibrium equations in each of the x and $y-$ directions:

   Noting that $T_{BC} = T_{BD} = T$ (Frictionless pulley), $\alpha = 10°$ and $\beta = 20°$, we have that

   $$+\rightarrow \ \sum F_x = 0: \quad -T\cos\beta + T\cos\alpha - T_{BA} = 0$$

   $$+\uparrow \ \sum F_y = 0: \quad T\sin\alpha + T\sin\beta - W = 0$$

6. Solve these equations to find the required tension in the line AB :

   $$T_{BA} = \left(\frac{\cos\alpha - \cos\beta}{\sin\alpha + \sin\beta}\right) W = 21.87 \ lb.$$

3.2 Free-Body Diagrams in the Equilibrium of a Rigid Body

In each of the following problems, assume that the objects are in equilibrium.

Problem 3.16.

Draw the free-body diagram of the 50-kg uniform bar supported at A and B.

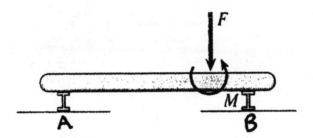

Solution

1. Imagine the bar to be separated or detached from the system.
2. The supports at A and B are equivalent to Roller Supports. Use Table 2.1 to determine the number and types of reactions *acting on the bar* at A and B.
3. The bar is subjected to four *external* forces (don't forget the weight!). They are caused by:

   i.   **ii.**

   iii.   **iv.**

   The bar is subjected also to one applied external couple moment with magnitude M.
4. Draw the free-body diagram of the (detached) bar showing all these forces and any couples labeled with their magnitudes and directions. *Assume* the sense of the vectors representing the *reactions acting on the bar* (the correct sense will always emerge from the equilibrium equations for the bar). Include any other relevant information e.g. lengths, angles etc which may help when formulating the equilibrium equations (including the moment equation) for the pipe.

Problem 3.16.

Draw the free-body diagram of the 50-kg uniform bar supported at A and B.

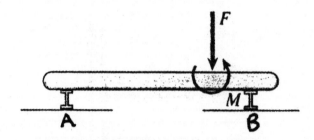

Solution

1. Imagine the bar to be separated or detached from the system.
2. The supports at A and B are equivalent to Roller Supports. Use Table 2.1 to determine the number and types of reactions *acting on the bar* at A and B.
3. The bar is subjected to four *external* forces (don't forget the weight!). They are caused by:

   i. REACTION AT A   **ii. REACTION AT B**

   iii. APPLIED FORCE F   **iv. WEIGHT OF BAR**

   The bar is subjected also to one applied external couple with magnitude M.
4. Draw the free-body diagram of the (detached) bar showing all these forces and any couples labeled with their magnitudes and directions. *Assume* the sense of the vectors representing the *reactions acting on the bar* (the correct sense will always emerge from the equilibrium equations for the bar). Include any other relevant information e.g. lengths, angles etc which may help when formulating the equilibrium equations (including the moment equation) for the pipe.

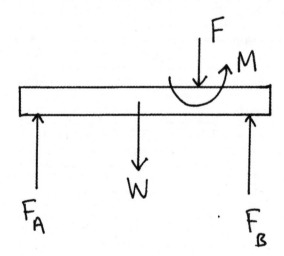

Problem 3.17.

Draw the free-body diagram of the bar which is built-in at A. Neglect the weight of the bar.

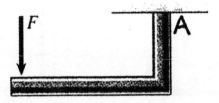

Solution

1. Imagine the bar to be separated or detached from the system.
2. The support at A is a built-in support. Use Table 2.1 to determine the number and types of reactions *acting on the bar* at A.
3. The bar is subjected to three *external* forces. They are caused by:

   i.   **ii.**

   iii.

   The bar is subjected to one *external* couple. It is caused by:

4. Draw the free-body diagram of the (detached) bar showing all these forces and any couples labeled with their magnitudes and directions. *Assume* the sense of the vectors representing the *reactions acting on the bar* (the correct sense will always emerge from the equilibrium equations for the bar). Include any other relevant information e.g. lengths, angles etc which may help when formulating the equilibrium equations (including the moment equation) for the bar.

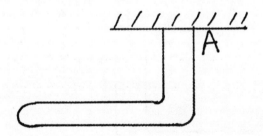

Problem 3.17.

Draw the free-body diagram of the bar which is built-in at A. Neglect the weight of the bar.

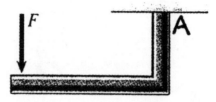

Solution

1. Imagine the bar to be separated or detached from the system.
2. The support at A is a built-in support. Use Table 2.1 to determine the number and types of reactions *acting on the bar* at A.
3. The bar is subjected to three *external* forces. They are caused by:

   i. REACTION AT A (2 forces)   **ii. APPLIED FORCE F**

   The bar is subjected to one *external* couple. It is caused by:
   REACTION AT A

4. Draw the free-body diagram of the (detached) bar showing all these forces and any couples labeled with their magnitudes and directions. *Assume* the sense of the vectors representing the *reactions acting on the bar* (the correct sense will always emerge from the equilibrium equations for the bar). Include any other relevant information e.g. lengths, angles etc which may help when formulating the equilibrium equations (including the moment equation) for the bar.

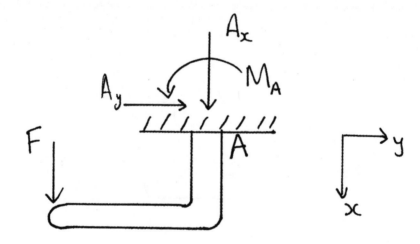

Problem 3.18.

Draw the free-body diagram of the beam which is supported by smooth surfaces at A and B and a rope at C. Neglect the weight of the beam.

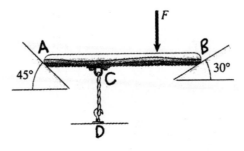

Solution

1. Imagine the beam to be separated or detached from the system.
2. The beam contacts the smooth surfaces at A and B and is supported additionally by a rope at C. Use Table 2.1 to determine the number and types of reactions *acting on the beam* at A, B and C.
3. The beam is subjected to four *external* forces. They are caused by:

   i.   **ii.**

   iii.   **iv.**

4. Draw the free-body diagram of the (detached) beam showing all these forces labeled with their magnitudes and directions. *Assume* the sense of the vectors representing the *reactions acting on the beam* (the correct sense will always emerge from the equilibrium equations for the beam). Include any other relevant information e.g. lengths, angles etc which may help when formulating the equilibrium equations (including the moment equation) for the beam.

Problem 3.18.

Draw the free-body diagram of the beam which is supported by smooth surfaces at *A* and *B* and a rope at *C*. Neglect the weight of the beam.

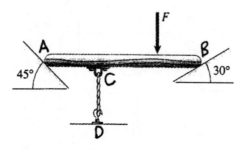

Solution

1. Imagine the beam to be separated or detached from the system.
2. The beam contacts the smooth surfaces at *A* and *B* and is supported additionally by a rope at *C*. Use Table 2.1 to determine the number and types of reactions *acting on the beam* at *A*, *B* and *C*.
3. The beam is subjected to four *external* forces. They are caused by:

   i. REACTION AT *A*   **ii. REACTION AT** *B*

   iii. APPLIED FORCE F   **iv. CORD** *C D*

4. Draw the free-body diagram of the (detached) beam showing all these forces labeled with their magnitudes and directions. *Assume* the sense of the vectors representing the *reactions acting on the beam* (the correct sense will always emerge from the equilibrium equations for the beam). Include any other relevant information e.g. lengths, angles etc which may help when formulating the equilibrium equations (including the moment equation) for the beam.

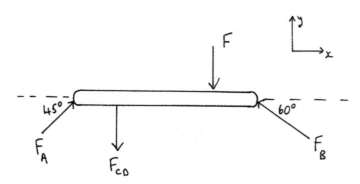

Problem 3.19.

Draw the free-body diagram of the plate which has a weight of 50 lb. The plate is supported by a pin connection at A and a constrained pin at B.

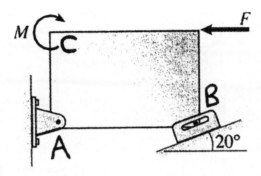

Solution

1. Imagine the plate to be separated or detached from its supports.
2. There is a pin support at A and and an inclined constrained pin support at B. Use Table 2.1 to determine the number and types of reactions *acting on the plate* at A and B.
3. The plate is subjected to five *external* forces. They are caused by:

   i.   **ii.**

   iii.   **iv.**

   v.

   In addition, the plate is subjected to one *external* applied couple of magnitude M at C.
4. Draw the free-body diagram of the (detached) plate showing all these forces and any couples labeled with their magnitudes and directions. *Assume* the sense of the vectors representing the *reactions acting on the plate* (the correct sense will always emerge from the equilibrium equations for the plate). Include any other relevant information e.g. lengths, angles etc which may help when formulating the equilibrium equations (including the moment equation) for the plate.

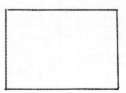

Problem 3.19.

Draw the free-body diagram of the plate which has a weight of 50 lb. The plate is supported by a pin connection at A and a constrained pin at B.

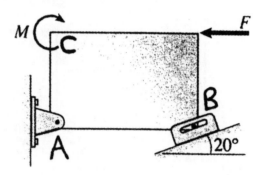

Solution

1. Imagine the plate to be separated or detached from its supports.
2. There is a pin support at A and and an inclined constrained pin support at B. Use Table 2.1 to determine the number and types of reactions *acting on the plate* at A and B.
3. The plate is subjected to five *external* forces.
    They are caused by:

    i. **REACTION AT** A **(2 forces)**   ii. **REACTION AT** B

    iii. **APPLIED FORCE F**   iv. **WEIGHT OF PLATE**

    In addition, the plate is subjected to one applied couple of magnitude M at C.

4. Draw the free-body diagram of the (detached) plate showing all these forces and any couples labeled with their magnitudes and directions. *Assume* the sense of the vectors representing the *reactions acting on the plate* (the correct sense will always emerge from the equilibrium equations for the plate). Include any other relevant information e.g. lengths, angles etc which may help when formulating the equilibrium equations (including the moment equation) for the plate.

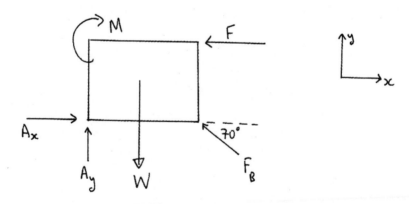

Problem 3.20.

Draw the free-body diagram of the link AC, which is (constrained-) pin-connected at A and rocker (roller) - supported at C. Neglect the weight of the link.

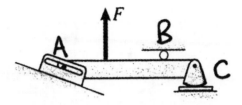

Solution

1. Imagine the link AC to be separated or detached from the system.

2. There is a pin connection at A, a rocker support at C and a roller support acts on the link at B. Use Table 2.1 to determine the number and types of reactions *acting on the link* at A, B and C.

3. The link is subjected to four *external* forces.
   They are caused by:

   i.   **ii.**

   iii.   **iv.**

4. Draw the free-body diagram of the (detached) link showing all these forces labeled with their magnitudes and directions. *Assume* the sense of the vectors representing the *reactions acting on the link* (the correct sense will always emerge from the equilibrium equations for the link). Include any other relevant information e.g. lengths, angles etc which may help when formulating the equilibrium equations (including the moment equation) for the link.

Problem 3.20.

Draw the free-body diagram of the link AC, which is (constrained-) pin-connected at A and rocker (roller) - supported at C. Neglect the weight of the link.

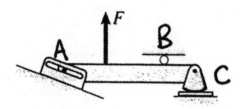

Solution

1. Imagine the link AC to be separated or detached from the system.
2. There is a pin connection at A, a rocker support at C and a roller support acts on the link at B. Use Table 2.1 to determine the number and types of reactions *acting on the link* at A, B and C.
3. The link is subjected to four *external* forces.
   They are caused by:

   i. **REACTION AT** A ii. **REACTION AT** B

   iii. **REACTION AT** C iv. **APPLIED FORCE F**

4. Draw the free-body diagram of the (detached) link showing all these forces labeled with their magnitudes and directions. *Assume* the sense of the vectors representing the *reactions acting on the link* (the correct sense will always emerge from the equilibrium equations for the link). Include any other relevant information e.g. lengths, angles etc which may help when formulating the equilibrium equations (including the moment equation) for the link.

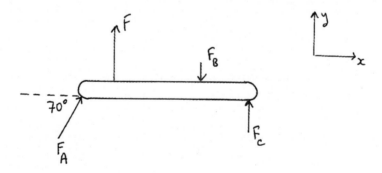

Problem 3.21.

Draw the free-body diagram of the uniform bar which has a mass of 10 kg and a center of mass at G. The bar contacts a rough surface at B.

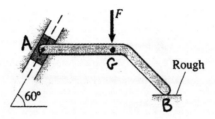

Solution

1. Imagine the bar to be separated or detached from the system.
2. The bar rests on a rough surface at B while end A is constrained by a slider. Use Table 2.1 to determine the number and types of reactions *acting on the bar* at A and B.
3. The bar is subjected to five *external* forces. They are caused by:

   i.   ii.

   iii.   iv.

   v.

4. Draw the free-body diagram of the (detached) bar showing all these forces labeled with their magnitudes and directions. *Assume* the sense of the vectors representing the *reactions acting on the bar* (the correct sense will always emerge from the equilibrium equations for the bar). Include any other relevant information e.g. lengths, angles etc which may help when formulating the equilibrium equations for the bar.

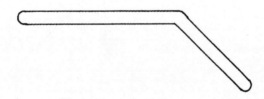

Problem 3.21.

Draw the free-body diagram of the uniform bar which has a mass of 10 kg and a center of mass at G. The bar contacts a rough surface at B.

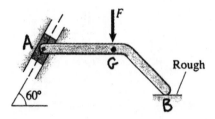

Solution

1. Imagine the bar to be separated or detached from the system.
2. The bar rests on a rough surface at B while end A is constrained by a slider. Use Table 2.1 to determine the number and types of reactions *acting on the bar* at A and B.
3. The bar is subjected to five *external* forces. They are caused by:

    i. REACTION AT B (2 forces)   **ii. REACTION AT A**

    iii. APPLIED FORCE F   **iv. WEIGHT OF BAR**

4. Draw the free-body diagram of the (detached) bar showing all these forces labeled with their magnitudes and directions. *Assume* the sense of the vectors representing the *reactions acting on the bar* (the correct sense will always emerge from the equilibrium equations for the bar). Include any other relevant information e.g. lengths, angles etc which may help when formulating the equilibrium equations for the bar.

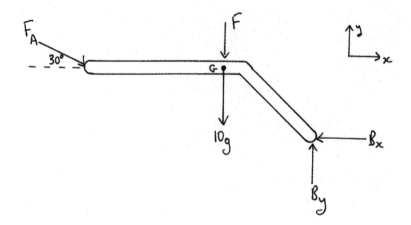

Problem 3.22.

In the following figure, the tension in cable AB is T. Draw a free-body diagram of the assembly and cable AB, treating them as a single object. Neglect the weight of the pipe assembly.

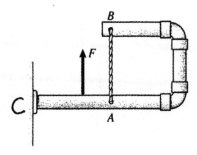

Solution

1. Imagine the entire pipe assembly to be separated or detached from the system (the supporting wall).
2. There is a built-in (fixed) support at C. Use Table 2.1 to determine the number and types of reactions *acting on the assembly* at C.
3. In addition to the force with magnitude F shown in the figure, the assembly is subjected to two additional *external* forces and an external couple. They are caused by:

   There are no other external forces acting on the assembly.
4. Draw the free-body diagram of the (detached) assembly showing all these forces and any couples labeled with their magnitudes and directions. *Assume* the sense of the vectors representing the *reactions acting on the assembly* (the correct sense will always emerge from the equilibrium equations for the assembly). Include any other relevant information e.g. lengths, angles etc which may help when formulating the equilibrium equations (including the moment equation) for the assembly.

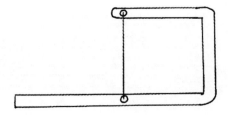

Problem 3.22.

In the following figure, the tension in cable AB is T. Draw a free-body diagram of the assembly and cable AB, treating them as a single object. Neglect the weight of the pipe assembly.

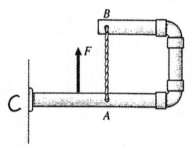

Solution

1. Imagine the entire pipe assembly to be separated or detached from the system (the supporting wall).
2. There is a built-in (fixed) support at C. Use Table 2.1 to determine the number and types of reactions *acting on the assembly* at C.
3. In addition to the force with magnitude F shown in the figure, the assembly is subjected to two additional *external* forces and an external couple. They are caused by:
   THE SUPPORT AT C
   There are no other external forces acting on the assembly.
4. Draw the free-body diagram of the (detached) assembly showing all these forces and any couples labeled with their magnitudes and directions. *Assume* the sense of the vectors representing the *reactions acting on the assembly* (the correct sense will always emerge from the equilibrium equations for the assembly). Include any other relevant information e.g. lengths, angles etc which may help when formulating the equilibrium equations (including the moment equation) for the assembly.

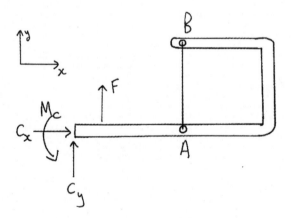

Problem 3.23.

Draw the free-body diagram of the assembly in **Problem 3.22** but this time *not* including cable AB.

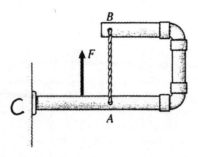

Solution

1. Imagine the assembly ABC to be separated or detached from the system (supporting wall + cable).
2. There is a built-in (fixed) support at C. As in Problem 3.22, use Table 2.1 to determine the number and types of reactions *acting on the assembly* at C. In addition to these reactions, we now have additional external forces acting on the assembly as a result of the tension in cable AB.
3. In addition to the force with magnitude F shown in the figure, the assembly is now, therefore, subjected to four *external* forces and an external couple. They are:

    i.   ii.

    iii.   iv.

    v.

4. Draw the free-body diagram of the (detached) assembly showing all these forces and any couples labeled with their magnitudes and directions. *Assume* the sense of the vectors representing the *reactions acting on the assembly* (the correct sense will always emerge from the equilibrium equations for the assembly). Include any other relevant information e.g. lengths, angles etc which may help when formulating the equilibrium equations (including the moment equation) for the assembly.

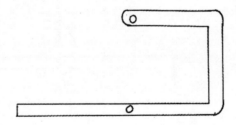

Problem 3.23.

Draw the free-body diagram of the assembly in **Problem 3.22** but this time *not* including cable AB.

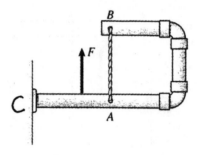

Solution

1. Imagine the assembly ABC to be separated or detached from the system (supporting wall + cable).
2. There is a built-in (fixed) support at C. As in Problem 3.22, use Table 2.1 to determine the number and types of reactions *acting on the assembly* at C. In addition to these reactions, we now have additional external forces acting on the assembly as a result of the tension in cable AB.
3. In addition to the force with magnitude F shown in the figure, the assembly is now, therefore, subjected to four *external* forces and an external couple. They are:

   i. (i) **REACTION AT** C **(2 forces and a couple)**   ii. **TWO TENSION (CABLE) FORCES (equal magnitude, opposite directions) ACTING ON THE BAR AT** A **and** B.

4. Draw the free-body diagram of the (detached) assembly showing all these forces and any couples labeled with their magnitudes and directions. *Assume* the sense of the vectors representing the *reactions acting on the assembly* (the correct sense will always emerge from the equilibrium equations for the assembly). Include any other relevant information e.g. lengths, angles etc which may help when formulating the equilibrium equations (including the moment equation) for the assembly.

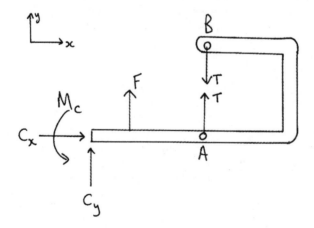

Problem 3.24.

Draw the free-body diagram of cable AB in the assembly of **Problem 3.22**.

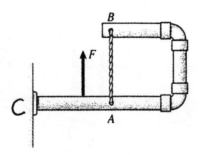

Solution

1. Imagine the cable to be separated or detached from the system.
2. The cable AB is subjected to two *external* forces. They are:

   i.   **ii.**

3. Draw the free-body diagram of the (detached) cable showing these forces labeled with their magnitudes and directions.

Problem 3.24.

Draw the free-body diagram of cable AB in the assembly of **Problem 3.22**.

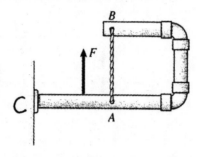

Solution

1. Imagine the cable to be separated or detached from the system.
2. The cable AB is subjected to two *external* forces. They are:
    i. **TWO TENSION FORCES (equal magnitude, opposite directions) ACTING ON THE CABLE AT** A and B. (These forces should be equal and opposite to the tension forces mentioned in Problem 3.23)
3. Draw the free-body diagram of the (detached) cable showing these forces labeled with their magnitudes and directions.

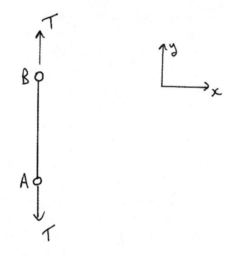

Problem 3.25.

The mass of the person is 80 kg and the mass of the diving board is 45 kg. Draw the free-body diagram of the diving board. Use the free-body diagram to write down equilibrium equations for the board and and to determine the reactions at the supports A and B.

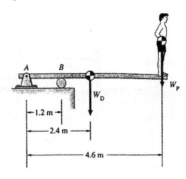

Solution

1. Imagine the diving board to be separated or detached from the system.

2. There is a pin support at A and a roller support at B. Use Table 2.1 to determine the number and types of reactions *acting on the board* at A and B.

3. The board is subjected to five *external* forces. They are caused by:

    i.   **ii.**

    iii.   **iv.**

    v.

4. Draw the free-body diagram of the (detached) board showing all these forces labeled with their magnitudes and directions. *Assume* the sense of the vectors representing the *reactions acting on the board* (the correct sense will always emerge from the equilibrium equations for the board). Include any other relevant information e.g. lengths, angles etc which may help when formulating the equilibrium equations (including the moment equation) for the board.

5. The weight of the person is: $W_P =$
   The weight of the diving board is: $W_D =$

6. Establish an xy-axes system on the free-body diagram and write down the force equilibrium equations in each of the x and $y-$ directions:

   $+\rightarrow \ \sum F_x = 0 :$

   $+\uparrow \ \sum F_y = 0 :$
   Sum moments about A and write down the moment equilibrium equation.

   $\curvearrowright + \sum M_A = 0 :$

7. Solve the three equations (using the values for W_P and W_D obtained above) for the required reactions at A and B.

Problem 3.25.

The mass of the person is 80 kg and the mass of the diving board is 45 kg. Draw the free-body diagram of the diving board. Use the free-body diagram to write down equilibrium equations for the board and and to determine the reactions at the supports A and B.

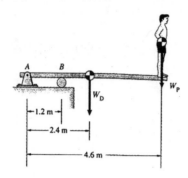

Solution

1. Imagine the diving board to be separated or detached from the system.
2. There is a pin support at A and a roller support at B. Use Table 2.1 to determine the number and types of reactions *acting on the board* at A and B.
3. The board is subjected to five *external* forces. They are caused by:

   i. **REACTION AT A (Two forces)**   ii. **REACTION AT B**

   iii. **WEIGHT OF PERSON (W_P)**   iv. **WEIGHT OF DIVING BOARD (W_D)**

4. Draw the free-body diagram of the (detached) board showing all these forces labeled with their magnitudes and directions. *Assume* the sense of the vectors representing the *reactions acting on the board* (the correct sense will always emerge from the equilibrium equations for the board). Include any other relevant information e.g. lengths, angles etc which may help when formulating the equilibrium equations (including the moment equation) for the board.

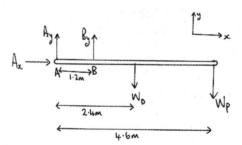

5. The weight of the person has magnitude: $W_P = mg = 80\,(9.8) = 784N$
   The weight of the diving board has magnitude: $W_D = mg = 45\,(9.8) = 441N$
6. Establish an xy-axes system on the free-body diagram and write down the force equilibrium equations in each of the x and $y-$ directions:

   $+\rightarrow \sum F_x = 0:\quad A_x = 0.$

   $+\uparrow\ \sum F_y = 0:\quad -W_P - W_D + B_y + A_y = 0.$
   Sum moments about A and write down the moment equilibrium equation.
   $\curvearrowright + \sum M_A = 0:\quad -4.6(784) - 2.4\,(441) + 1.2B_y = 0.$
7. Solve the three equations (using the values for W_P and W_D obtained above) for the required reactions at A and B :
   $B_y = 3887.3N, A_y = -2662.3N$ (directions as shown on the FBD).

Problem 3.26.

Draw the free-body diagram of the beam and use it to determine the reactions at the support A. Neglect the weight of the beam.

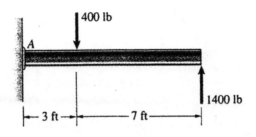

Solution

1. Imagine the beam to be separated or detached from the system (wall).
2. There is a built-in support at A. Use Table 2.1 to determine the number and types of reactions *acting on the beam* at A.
3. The beam is subjected to four *external* forces and an external couple. They are:

   i.   **ii.**

   iii.   **iv.**

   v.

4. Draw the free-body diagram of the (detached) beam showing all these forces and the external couple labeled with their magnitudes and directions. *Assume* the sense of the vectors representing the *reactions acting on the beam* (the correct sense will always emerge from the equilibrium equations for the beam). Include any other relevant information e.g. lengths, angles etc which may help when formulating the equilibrium equations (including the moment equation) for the beam.

5. Establish an xy-axes system on the free-body diagram and write down the force equilibrium equations in each of the x and $y-$ directions:

   $$+\rightarrow \sum F_x = 0:$$

   $$+\uparrow \ \sum F_y = 0:$$

   Sum moments about A and write down the moment equilibrium equation.

   $$\curvearrowright +\sum M_A = 0:$$

6. Solve the three equations for the required reactions at the support A.

Problem 3.26.

Draw the free-body diagram of the beam and use it to determine the reactions at the support A. Neglect the weight of the beam.

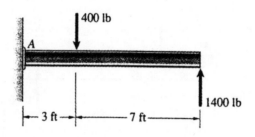

Solution

1. Imagine the beam to be separated or detached from the system (wall).
2. There is a built-in support at A. Use Table 2.1 to determine the number and types of reactions *acting on the beam* at A.
3. The beam is subjected to four *external* forces and an external couple. They are:

   i. REACTIONS AT A (Two forces and a couple)   **ii.** 400 lb **LOAD**

   iii. 1400 lb **LOAD**

4. Draw the free-body diagram of the (detached) beam showing all these forces and the external couple labeled with their magnitudes and directions. *Assume* the sense of the vectors representing the *reactions acting on the beam* (the correct sense will always emerge from the equilibrium equations for the beam). Include any other relevant information e.g. lengths, angles etc which may help when formulating the equilibrium equations (including the moment equation) for the beam.

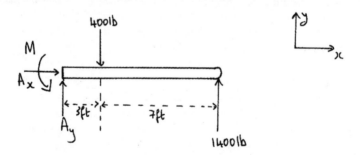

5. Establish an xy-axes system on the free-body diagram and write down the force equilibrium equations in each of the x and $y-$ directions:

   $$+\rightarrow \sum F_x = 0: \quad A_x = 0.$$

   $$+\uparrow \ \sum F_y = 0: \quad A_y - 400 + 1400 = 0.$$

   Sum moments about A and write down the moment equilibrium equation.

   $$\curvearrowleft + \sum M_A = 0: \quad M - 3\,(400) + 10\,(1400) = 0$$

6. Solve the three equations for the required reactions at the support A :

   $A_y = -1000$ lb, $M = -12800$ ft.lb (directions as shown on the FBD).

Problem 3.27.

Draw a free-body diagram of the beam.

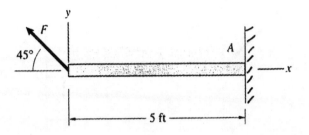

Solution

1. Imagine the beam to be separated or detached from the system.
2. There is a built-in (fixed) support at A. Use Table 2.1 to determine the number and types of reactions *acting on the beam* at A.
3. The beam is subjected to four *external* forces and one external couple. They are caused by:

4. Draw the free-body diagram of the (detached) beam showing all these forces and the couple labeled with their magnitudes and directions. *Assume* the sense of the vectors representing the *reactions acting on the beam*. Include any other relevant information e.g. lengths, angles etc which may help when formulating the equilibrium equations (including the moment equation) for the beam.

Problem 3.27.

Draw a free-body diagram of the beam.

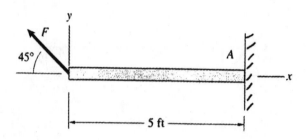

Solution

1. Imagine the beam to be separated or detached from the system.
2. There is a built-in (fixed) support at A. Use Table 2.1 to determine the number and types of reactions *acting on the beam* at A.
3. The beam is subjected to four *external* forces and one external couple. They are caused by:

   i. REACTION AT A (Two forces and a couple).   **ii. APPLIED FORCE F.**

   iii. WEIGHT OF BAR.

4. Draw the free-body diagram of the (detached) beam showing all these forces and the couple labeled with their magnitudes and directions. *Assume* the sense of the vectors representing the *reactions acting on the beam*. Include any other relevant information e.g. lengths, angles etc which may help when formulating the equilibrium equations (including the moment equation) for the beam.

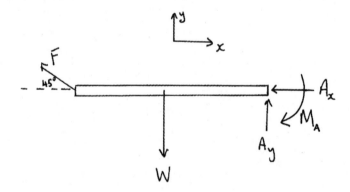

Problem 3.28.

The mobile is in equilibrium. The weights of the crossbars are negligible. Draw free-body diagrams for each of the crossbars.

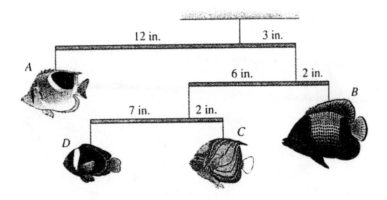

Solution

1. Imagine each crossbar to be separated or detached from the system.
2. Each crossbar has the reaction from a cable support and two weights acting externally. Be careful - not all of these forces are independent!
3. Draw the free-body diagram of each (detached) crossbar showing all these forces labeled with their magnitudes and directions. Include any other relevant information e.g. lengths, angles etc which may help when formulating the equilibrium equations (including the moment equation) for each crossbar.

Problem 3.28.

The mobile is in equilibrium. The weights of the crossbars are negligible. Draw free-body diagrams for each of the crossbars.

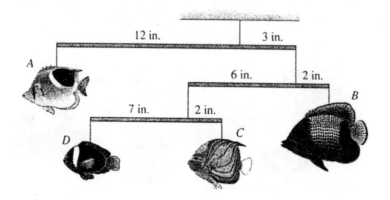

Solution

1. Imagine each crossbar to be separated or detached from the system.
2. Each crossbar has the reaction from a cable support and two weights acting externally. Be careful - not all of these forces are independent!
3. Draw the free-body diagram of each (detached) crossbar showing all these forces labeled with their magnitudes and directions. Include any other relevant information e.g. lengths, angles etc which may help when formulating the equilibrium equations (including the moment equation) for each crossbar.

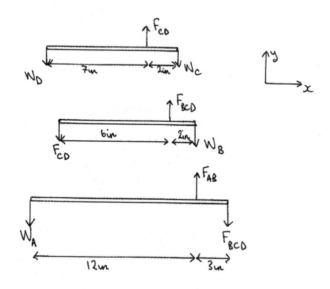

F_{AB}, F_{CD}, F_{BCD} : Magnitudes of reactions at the supports

W_A, W_B, W_C, W_D : Weights of A, B, C and D, respectively.

Problem 3.29.

The lift forces on an airplane's wing are represented by eight forces. The magnitude of each force is given in terms of its position x on the wing by $F_L = 200\sqrt{1 - (x/17)^2}$ lb. The weight of the wing is $W = 400$ lb. Draw a free-body diagram for the wing and use it to formulate equilibrium equations for the wing. Solve these equilibrium equations to find the reactions on the wing at the root R.

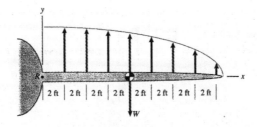

Solution

1. Imagine the wing to be separated or detached from the system (airplane).
2. There is a built-in support at R. Use Table 2.1 to determine the number and types of reactions *acting on the wing* at R.
3. Apart from the lift forces, the wing is subjected to three *external* forces and an external couple. They are caused by:
4. Draw the free-body diagram of the (detached) wing showing all these forces and the external couple labeled with their magnitudes and directions. *Assume* the sense of the vectors representing the *reactions acting on the wing* (the correct sense will always emerge from the equilibrium equations for the wing). Include any other relevant information e.g. lengths, angles etc which may help when formulating the equilibrium equations (including the moment equation) for the wing.

5. Make a table showing the magnitudes of the forces and the moments about the wing root R acting on the wing.

Station	Distance D (ft.)	Force Magnitude F_L	Moment Magnitude M_L
1	2		
2	4		
3	6		
4	8		
5	10		
6	12		
7	14		
8	16		
Sum			

6. Establish an $xy-$axes system on the free-body diagram and write down the force equilibrium equations in each of the x and $y-$ directions:

$$+\rightarrow \sum F_x = 0:$$

$$+\uparrow \ \sum F_y = 0:$$

Sum moments about R and write down the moment equilibrium equation.

$$\curvearrowright +\sum M_R = 0:$$

7. Solve the three equations for the required reactions at the support R.

Problem 3.29.

The lift forces on an airplane's wing are represented by eight forces. The magnitude of each force is given in terms of its position x on the wing by $F_L = 200\sqrt{1 - (x/17)^2}$ lb. The weight of the wing is $W = 400$ lb. Draw a free-body diagram for the wing and use it to formulate equilibrium equations for the wing. Solve these equilibrium equations to find the reactions on the wing at the root R.

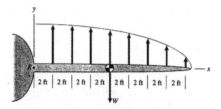

Solution

1. Imagine the wing to be separated or detached from the system (airplane).
2. There is a built-in support at R. Use Table 2.1 to determine the number and types of reactions *acting on the wing* at R.
3. Apart from the lift forces, the wing is subjected to three *external* forces and an external couple. They are caused by:

   i. THE BUILT-IN SUPPORT AT R (two forces and a cou-ii. WEIGHT OF THE WING. ple).

4. Draw the free-body diagram of the (detached) wing showing all these forces and the external couple labeled with their magnitudes and directions. *Assume* the sense of the vectors representing the *reactions acting on the wing* (the correct sense will always emerge from the equilibrium equations for the wing). Include any other relevant information e.g. lengths, angles etc which may help when formulating the equilibrium equations (including the moment equation) for the wing.

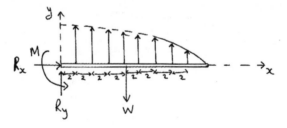

5. Make a table showing the magnitudes of the forces and the moments about the wing root R acting on the wing.

Station	Distance D (ft.)	Force Magnitude F_L	Moment Magnitude M_L
1	2	198.61	397.22
2	4	194.38	777.54
3	6	187.13	1122.78
4	8	176.47	1411.76
5	10	161.74	1617.38
6	12	141.67	1700.0
7	14	113.45	1588.37
8	16	67.58	1081.33
Sum $\sum$		1241.03	9696.40

6. Establish an xy−axes system on the free-body diagram and write down the force equilibrium equations in each of the x and $y-$ directions:

   $+\rightarrow \ \sum F_x = 0 :$ $R_x = 0.$
   $+\uparrow \ \sum F_y = 0 :$ $R_y + \sum F_L - W = 0.$

   Sum moments about R and write down the moment equilibrium equation.

   $\curvearrowleft + \sum M_R = 0 :$ $M + \sum M_L - 8W = 0.$

7. Solve the three equations for the required reactions at the support R :

   $R_x = 0, R_y = -841$ lb, $M = -6496.3$ ft.lb (directions as shown on FBD).

Problem 3.30.

The weight W of the bar acts at its center. The surfaces are smooth. Draw a free-body diagram of the bar and use it to write down equilibrium equations for the bar.

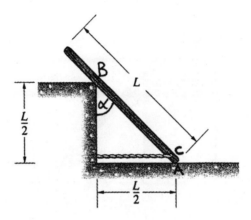

Solution

1. Imagine the bar to be separated or detached from the system.
2. The supports at A and B are contacts with a smooth surface. There is also a cable support at C. Use Table 2.1 to identify the reactions *acting on the bar* at A, B and C.
3. The bar is subjected to four *external* forces.
4. Draw the free-body diagram of the (detached) bar showing all these forces labeled with their magnitudes and directions. *Assume* the sense of the vectors representing the *reactions acting on the bar*. Include any other relevant information e.g. lengths, angles etc which may help when formulating the equilibrium equations (including the moment equation) for the bar.
5. On the free-body diagram, establish an $xy-$axes system and resolve all forces into x and y components.

6. Write down the force equilibrium equations in each of the x and $y-$ directions
$$+\rightarrow \ \sum F_x = 0 :$$

$$+\uparrow \ \sum F_y = 0 :$$
7. Sum moments about A and write down the moment equilibrium equation.
$$\curvearrowleft + \sum M_A = 0 :$$

Problem 3.30.

The weight W of the bar acts at its center. The surfaces are smooth. Draw a free-body diagram of the bar and use it to write down equilibrium equations for the bar.

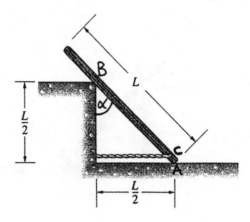

Solution

1. Imagine the bar to be separated or detached from the system.
2. The supports at A and B are contacts with a smooth surface. There is also a cable support at C. Use Table 2.1 to identify the reactions *acting on the bar* at A, B and C.
3. The bar is subjected to four *external* forces.
4. Draw the free-body diagram of the (detached) bar showing all these forces labeled with their magnitudes and directions. *Assume* the sense of the vectors representing the *reactions acting on the bar*. Include any other relevant information e.g. lengths, angles etc which may help when formulating the equilibrium equations (including the moment equation) for the bar.
5. On the free-body diagram, establish an $xy-$axes system and resolve all forces into x and y components.

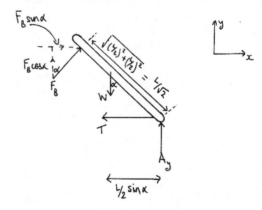

6. Write down the force equilibrium equations in each of the x and $y-$ directions (noting that $\alpha = 45°$):

$$+\rightarrow \ \sum F_x = 0: \quad -T + F_B \sin\alpha = 0 \Leftrightarrow -T + \frac{F_B}{\sqrt{2}} = 0.$$

$$+\uparrow \ \sum F_y = 0: \quad -W + A_y + F_B \cos\alpha = 0 \Leftrightarrow -W + A_y + \frac{F_B}{\sqrt{2}} = 0.$$

7. Sum moments about A and write down the moment equilibrium equation.

$$\curvearrowright +\sum M_A = 0: \quad \frac{WL}{2}\sin\alpha - \frac{F_B L}{\sqrt{2}} = 0 \Leftrightarrow \frac{WL}{2\sqrt{2}} + \frac{F_B L}{\sqrt{2}} = 0.$$

Problem 3.31.

The bar weighs W lb and its weight acts at its midpoint. The bar is unstretched when $\alpha = 0°$ and in equilibrium when $\alpha = \alpha_1°$. Draw a free-body diagram of the bar and use it to write down equilibrium equations for the bar.

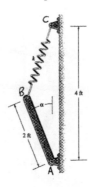

Solution

1. Imagine the bar to be separated or detached from the system.
2. The support at B is a pin support. Use Table 2.1 to identify the reactions *acting on the bar* at B. The bar is also acted upon by a spring force which acts along the line BC.
3. The bar is subjected to four *external* forces.
4. Draw the free-body diagram of the (detached) bar showing all these forces labeled with their magnitudes and directions. *Assume* the sense of the vectors representing the *reactions acting on the bar*. Include any other relevant information e.g. lengths, angles etc which may help when formulating the equilibrium equations (including the moment equation) for the bar.
5. On the free-body diagram, establish an $xy-$axes system and resolve all forces into x and y components.

6. Sum moments about A and write down the moment equilibrium equation.
$$\curvearrowleft + \sum M_A = 0 :$$
7. Write down the force equilibrium equations in each of the x and $y-$ directions
$$+\rightarrow \sum F_x = 0 :$$
$$+\uparrow \;\; \sum F_y = 0 :$$

Problem 3.31.

The bar weighs W lb and its weight acts at its midpoint. The bar is unstretched when $\alpha = 0°$ and in equilibrium when $\alpha = \alpha_1°$. Draw a free-body diagram of the bar and use it to write down equilibrium equations for the bar.

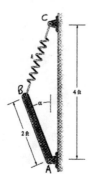

Solution

1. Imagine the bar to be separated or detached from the system.
2. The support at A is a pin support. Use Table 2.1 to identify the reactions *acting on the bar* at A. The bar is also acted upon by a spring force which acts along the line BC.
3. The bar is subjected to four *external* forces.
4. Draw the free-body diagram of the (detached) bar showing all these forces labeled with their magnitudes and directions. *Assume* the sense of the vectors representing the *reactions acting on the bar*. Include any other relevant information e.g. lengths, angles etc which may help when formulating the equilibrium equations (including the moment equation) for the bar.
5. On the free-body diagram, establish an $xy-$axes system and resolve all forces into x and y components.

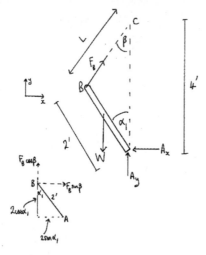

6. Write down the force equilibrium equations in each of the x and $y-$ directions
$$+\rightarrow \ \Sigma F_x = 0: \quad -A_x + F_B \sin\beta = 0.$$
$$+\uparrow \ \Sigma F_y = 0: \quad A_y + F_B \cos\beta - W = 0.$$
7. Sum moments about A and write down the moment equilibrium equation.
$$\curvearrowright +\Sigma M_A = 0: \quad W(1)\sin\alpha_1 - (F_B \sin\beta)(2)\cos\alpha_1 - (F_B \cos\beta)(2)\sin\alpha_1 = 0.$$

We note that the angle β is given by the law of sines as (see FBD): $\dfrac{\sin\alpha_1}{L} = \dfrac{\sin\beta}{2}$,

where $L = \sqrt{2^2 + 4^2 - 2(2)(4)\cos\alpha_1}$ is the stretched length of the spring (the distance from B to C when the bar is in equilibrium i.e. when $\alpha = \alpha_1°$).

Problem 3.32.

Use a free-body diagram of the bar AB to write down the equilibrium equations for the bar. Hence, find the tension in the cable and the reactions at A. The weight $W = 1.2kN$.

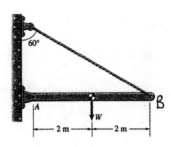

Solution

1. There is a pin support at A and a cable support at B. Draw the free-body diagram of the bar showing all external forces labeled with their magnitudes and directions. Include any other relevant information e.g. lengths, angles etc which may help when formulating the equilibrium equations (including the moment equation).

2. Establish an xy-axes system on the free-body diagram and write down the force equilibrium equations in each of the x and $y-$ directions

$$+\rightarrow \sum F_x = 0 :$$

$$+\uparrow \ \sum F_y = 0 :$$

3. Sum moments about a suitable point P and write down the moment equilibrium equation.

$$\curvearrowright + \sum M_P = 0 :$$

4. Solve the resulting three equilibrium equations simultaneously for the tension in the cable and the reactions at A.

Problem 3.32.

Use a free-body diagram of the bar AB to write down the equilibrium equations for the bar. Hence, find the tension in the cable and the reactions at A. The weight $W = 1.2kN$.

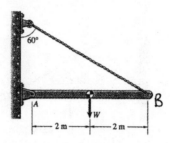

Solution

1. There is a pin support at A and a cable support at B. Draw the free-body diagram of the bar showing all external forces labeled with their magnitudes and directions. Include any other relevant information e.g. lengths, angles etc which may help when formulating the equilibrium equations (including the moment equation).

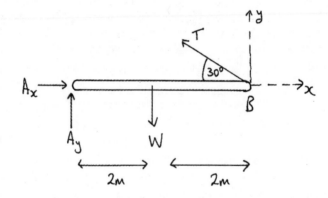

2. Establish an xy-axes system on the free-body diagram and write down the force equilibrium equations in each of the x and $y-$ directions.
$$+\rightarrow \; \sum F_x = 0: \quad A_x - T\cos 30° = 0$$
$$+\uparrow \; \sum F_y = 0: \quad A_y + T\sin 30° - W = 0$$
3. Sum moments about a suitable point P and write down the moment equilibrium equation.
   Sum moments about point B :
   $$\curvearrowleft + \sum M_B = 0: \quad 2W - 4A_y = 0$$
4. Solve the resulting three equilibrium equations simultaneously for the tension in the cable and the reactions at A :
   $$A_y = 0.6 \, kN, \quad T = 1.2 \, kN, \quad A_x = 1.0392 \, kN.$$

Problem 3.33.

The weight $W = 1000$ lb. Use a free-body diagram of the bar AB to write down the equilibrium equations for the bar. Hence, find the tension in the cable and the reactions at A. Assume the pulley is frictionless.

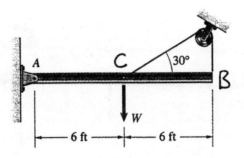

Solution

1. Identify all the external forces and couples acting on the detached bar. Use Table 2.1 to help with the support reactions (remember that a frictionless pulley changes the direction of a force but not its magnitude). Draw the free-body diagram of the detached bar showing all external forces and couples labeled with their magnitudes and directions. Include any other relevant information e.g. lengths, angles etc which may help when formulating the equilibrium equations (including the moment equation).

2. Establish an xy-axes system on the free-body diagram and write down the force equilibrium equations in each of the x and $y-$ directions

$$+\rightarrow \sum F_x = 0:$$

$$+\uparrow \ \sum F_y = 0:$$

3. Sum moments about a suitable point P and write down the moment equilibrium equation.

$$\curvearrowright +\sum M_P = 0:$$

4. Solve the resulting three equilibrium equations simultaneously for the tension in the cable and the reactions at A.

Problem 3.33.

The weight $W = 1000$ lb. Use a free-body diagram of the bar AB to write down the equilibrium equations for the bar. Hence, find the tension in the cable and the reactions at A. Assume the pulley is frictionless.

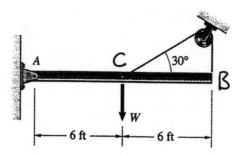

Solution

1. Identify all the external forces and couples acting on the detached bar. Use Table 2.1 to help with the support reactions (remember that a frictionless pulley changes the direction of a force but not its magnitude). Draw the free-body diagram of the detached bar showing all external forces and couples labeled with their magnitudes and directions. Include any other relevant information e.g. lengths, angles etc which may help when formulating the equilibrium equations (including the moment equation).

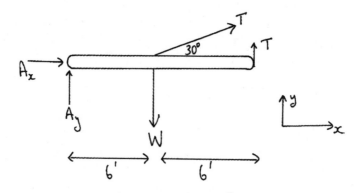

2. Establish an xy-axes system on the free-body diagram and write down the force equilibrium equations in each of the x and $y-$ directions.

$+\rightarrow \sum F_x = 0: \quad A_x + T\cos 30° = 0$

$+\uparrow \sum F_y = 0: \quad A_y + T\sin 30° - W + T = 0$

3. Sum moments about a suitable point P and write down the moment equilibrium equation.

   Sum moments about point A :

   $\curvearrowleft + \sum M_A = 0: \quad -6W + 6T\sin 30° + 12T = 0$

4. Solve the resulting three equilibrium equations simultaneously for the tension in the cable and the reactions at A :

   $A_x = -364.4$ lb, $T = 400$ lb, $A_y = 400$ lb.

Problem 3.34.

The distance $x = 3$ ft and the bar's weight is $W = 100$ lb. Use a free-body diagram of the bar AB to write down the equilibrium equations for the bar. Hence, find the tension in the cable and the reactions at A and B.

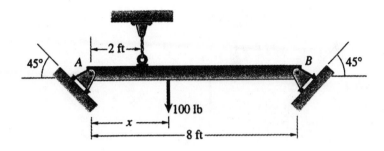

Solution

1. Identify all the external forces and couples acting on the detached bar. Use Table 2.1 to help with the support reactions. Draw the free-body diagram of the detached bar showing all external forces and couples labeled with their magnitudes and directions. Include any other relevant information e.g. lengths, angles etc which may help when formulating the equilibrium equations (including the moment equation).

2. Establish an xy-axes system on the free-body diagram and write down the force equilibrium equations in each of the x and $y-$ directions

$$+\rightarrow \sum F_x = 0 :$$

$$+\uparrow \ \sum F_y = 0 :$$

3. Sum moments about a suitable point P and write down the moment equilibrium equation.

$$\curvearrowleft + \sum M_P = 0 :$$

4. Solve the resulting three equilibrium equations simultaneously for the tension in the cable and the reactions at A and B.

Problem 3.34.

The distance $x = 3$ ft and the bar's weight is $W = 100$ lb. Use a free-body diagram of the bar AB to write down the equilibrium equations for the bar. Hence, find the tension in the cable and the reactions at A and B.

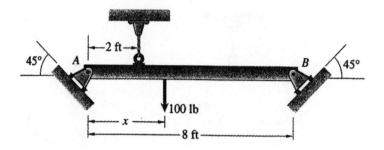

Solution

1. Identify all the external forces and couples acting on the detached bar. Use Table 2.1 to help with the support reactions. Draw the free-body diagram of the detached bar showing all external forces and couples labeled with their magnitudes and directions. Include any other relevant information e.g. lengths, angles etc which may help when formulating the equilibrium equations (including the moment equation).

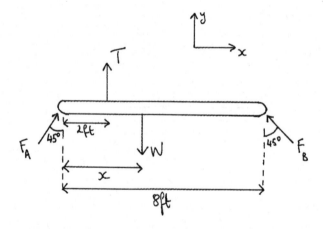

2. Establish an xy-axes system on the free-body diagram and write down the force equilibrium equations in each of the x and $y-$ directions.

   $+\rightarrow \sum F_x = 0:$ $F_A \sin 45° - F_B \sin 45° = 0$ i.e. $F_A = F_B$.

   $+\uparrow \sum F_y = 0:$ $F_A \cos 45° + F_B \cos 45° - W + T = 0$

3. Sum moments about a suitable point P and write down the moment equilibrium equation.

   Sum moments about point A :

   $\curvearrowleft + \sum M_A = 0:$ $2T - xW + 8F_B \cos 45° = 0$

4. Solve the resulting three equilibrium equations simultaneously for the tension in the cable and the reactions at A and B:

   Let $x = 3$ ft and $W = 100$ lb and solve the three simultaneous equations for the unknowns T, F_A and F_B :

   $F_A = F_B = 35.4$ lb, $T = 50$ lb.

Problem 3.35.

The crane's arm has a pin support at A. The hydraulic cylinder BC exerts a force on the arm at C in the direction parallel to BC. The crane's arm has a mass of m_C kg and its weight can be assume to act at a point 2 m to the right of A. The mass of the suspended box is m_B kg. The system is in equilibrium. Draw a free-body diagram of the crane's arm.

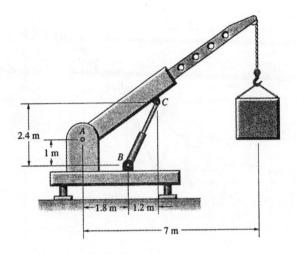

Solution

1. Imagine the arm to be separated or detached from the system.
2. Draw the free-body diagram of the (detached) arm showing all the external forces *acting on the arm* labeled with their magnitudes and directions. Include any other relevant information e.g. lengths, angles etc which may help when formulating the equilibrium equations (including the moment equation) for the arm. Establish an xy-axes system on the free-body diagram and use it to resolve any forces in the x and $y-$ directions.

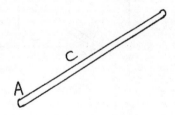

Problem 3.35.

The crane's arm has a pin support at A. The hydraulic cylinder BC exerts a force on the arm at C in the direction parallel to BC. The crane's arm has a mass of m_C kg and its weight can be assume to act at a point 2 m to the right of A. The mass of the suspended box is m_B kg. The system is in equilibrium. Draw a free-body diagram of the crane's arm.

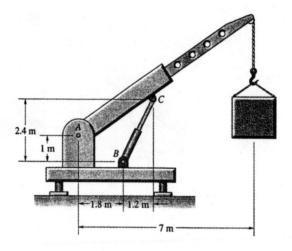

Solution

1. Imagine the arm to be separated or detached from the system.
2. Draw the free-body diagram of the (detached) arm showing all the external forces *acting on the arm* labeled with their magnitudes and directions. Include any other relevant information e.g. lengths, angles etc which may help when formulating the equilibrium equations (including the moment equation) for the arm. Establish an xy-axes system on the free-body diagram and use it to resolve any forces in the x and $y-$ directions.

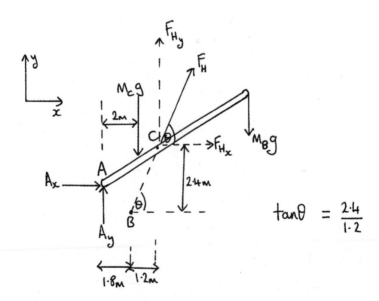

Problem 3.36.

Assume that a, b, M and k are known. The spring would be unstretched at $h = 0$. The system is in equilibrium when $h = h_0$ (known) and the beam is horizontal. Draw a free-body diagram of the beam which is assumed to have negligible weight and thickness. Use this free-body diagram to formulate equilibrium equations for the beam. Do you have the same number of equations as unknowns? Explain.

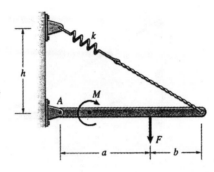

Solution

1. Identify all the external forces and couples acting on the detached beam. Use Table 2.1 to help with the support reactions. Draw the free-body diagram of the detached beam showing all external forces and couples labeled with their magnitudes and directions. Include any other relevant information e.g. lengths, angles etc which may help when formulating the equilibrium equations (including the moment equation).

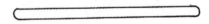

2. Establish an xy-axes system on the free-body diagram and write down the force equilibrium equations in each of the x and $y-$ directions:

$$+\rightarrow \sum F_x = 0:$$

$$+\uparrow \ \sum F_y = 0:$$

3. Sum moments about a suitable point P and write down the moment equilibrium equation.

$$\curvearrowleft + \sum M_P = 0:$$

4. You should now have three equilibrium equations involving four unknown variables (recall that a, b, M and k are known). Explain how one of these unknowns can be eliminated.

Problem 3.36.

Assume that a, b, M and k are known. The spring would be unstretched at $h = 0$. The system is in equilibrium when $h = h_0$ (known) and the beam is horizontal. Draw a free-body diagram of the beam which is assumed to have negligible weight and thickness. Use this free-body diagram to formulate equilibrium equations for the beam. Do you have the same number of equations as unknowns? Explain.

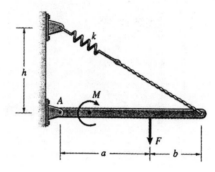

Solution

1. Identify all the external forces and couples acting on the detached beam. Use Table 2.1 to help with the support reactions. Draw the free-body diagram of the detached beam showing all external forces and couples labeled with their magnitudes and directions. Include any other relevant information e.g. lengths, angles etc which may help when formulating the equilibrium equations (including the moment equation).

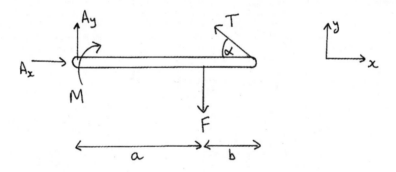

2. Establish an xy-axes system on the free-body diagram and write down the force equilibrium equations in each of the x and $y-$ directions:

$$+\rightarrow \sum F_x = 0: \quad A_x - T\cos\alpha° = 0.$$
$$+\uparrow \sum F_y = 0: \quad A_y - F + T\sin\alpha° = 0$$

3. Sum moments about a suitable point P and write down the moment equilibrium equation.

We sum moments about point A :

$$\curvearrowleft +\sum M_A = 0: \quad -M - aF + (a+b)\,T\sin\alpha° = 0$$

We note that $\alpha = \tan^{-1}(\frac{h_0}{a+b})$ which is known.

4. You should now have three equilibrium equations involving four unknown variables (recall that a, b, M and k are known). Explain how one of these unknowns can be eliminated:

We can obtain the magnitude T of the force exerted by the spring by using the relation $T = k\Delta L$ where ΔL is the stretch in the spring from equilibrium i.e. $\Delta L = \sqrt{h_0^2 + (a+b)^2} - (a+b)$.

Problem 3.37.

Draw the free-body diagram of the plate and show that the plate is statically indeterminate.

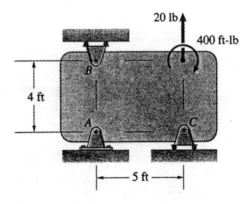

Solution

1. Imagine the plate to be separated or detached from the system.
2. Use Table 2.1 to determine the number and types of reactions *acting on the plate* at A, B and C.
3. Draw the free-body diagram of the (detached) plate showing all the external forces and couples *acting on the plate* labeled with their magnitudes and directions. *Assume* the sense of the vectors representing the *reactions acting on the plate*. Include any other relevant information e.g. lengths, angles etc which may help when formulating the equilibrium equations (including the moment equation) for the plate

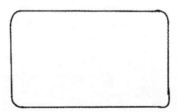

4. Compare the number of unknowns to the number of equilibrium conditions available and conclude that the plate is statically indeterminate.

Problem 3.37.

Draw the free-body diagram of the plate and show that the plate is statically indeterminate.

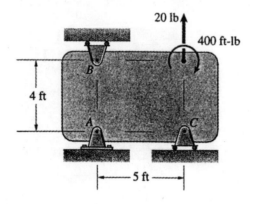

Solution

1. Imagine the plate to be separated or detached from the system.
2. Use Table 2.1 to determine the number and types of reactions *acting on the plate* at A, B and C.
3. Draw the free-body diagram of the (detached) plate showing all the external forces and couples *acting on the plate* labeled with their magnitudes and directions. *Assume* the sense of the vectors representing the *reactions acting on the plate.* Include any other relevant information e.g. lengths, angles etc which may help when formulating the equilibrium equations (including the moment equation) for the plate

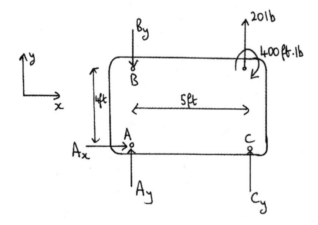

4. Compare the number of unknowns to the number of equilibrium conditions available and conclude that the plate is statically indeterminate.:
   There are three (equilibrium) equations and four unknown variables (A_x, A_y, B_y and C_y). Two unknowns ($A_x = 0$ and $C_y = 60$ lb)can be determined from two of the equilibrium equations but A_y and B_y are indeterminate.

Problem 3.38.

Consider the plate in **Problem 3.37**. Change one of the supports so that the plate is no longer statically indeterminate. Draw the new free-body diagram and use it to prove (by finding the reactions at the supports) that the plate is no longer statically indeterminate.

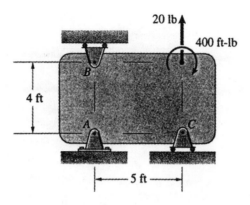

Solution

1. With three supports, each can have no more than one reaction. This means that we have to change the support at A accordingly. Pick one.

2. Draw the free-body diagram of the newly supported (detached) plate showing all the external forces and couples *acting on the plate* labeled with their magnitudes and directions.

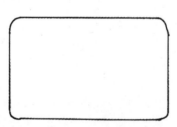

3. Compare the number of unknowns to the number of equilibrium conditions available and conclude that the plate is now statically determinate. To make sure:

4. Sum moments about point A and write down the moment equilibrium equation.

$$\curvearrowright + \sum M_A = 0:$$

5. Establish an xy-axes system on the free-body diagram and write down the force equilibrium equations in the x and $y-$ directions:

$$+\rightarrow \sum F_x = 0:$$

$$+\uparrow \; \sum F_y = 0:$$

6. Now solve these equations for the reactions at the supports.

Problem 3.38.

Consider the plate in **Problem 3.37**. Change one of the supports so that the plate is no longer statically indeterminate. Draw the new free-body diagram and use it to prove (by finding the reactions at the supports) that the plate is no longer statically indeterminate.

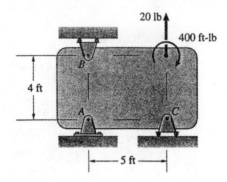

Solution

1. With three supports, each can have no more than one reaction. This means that we have to change the support at A accordingly. Pick one:

   Replace the pin support at A with an x−direction roller support.

2. Draw the free-body diagram of the newly supported (detached) plate showing all the external forces and couples *acting on the plate* labeled with their magnitudes and directions.

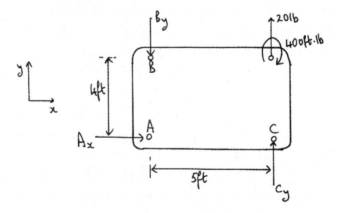

3. Compare the number of unknowns to the number of equilibrium conditions available and conclude that the plate is now statically determinate.

   (**3 equations and 3 unknowns**). To make sure:

4. Sum moments about point A and write down the moment equilibrium equation.

   $$\curvearrowleft + \sum M_A = 0: \quad -400 + 5\,(20) + 5C_y = 0.$$

5. Establish an xy-axes system on the free-body diagram and write down the force equilibrium equations in the x and $y−$ directions:

   $$+\rightarrow \ \sum F_x = 0: \quad A_x = 0.$$
   $$+\uparrow \ \sum F_y = 0: \quad C_y - B_y + 20 = 0.$$

6. Now solve these equations for the reactions at the supports:

   $$A_x = 0, \quad B_y = 80 \text{ lb}, \quad C_y = 60 \text{ lb}.$$

Problem 3.39.

The Howe bridge truss supports loads at F and G.
 (a) Draw the free-body diagram of the entire truss and use it to determine the reactions at the supports A and E.
 (b) Obtain a section by cutting members CD, CH and GH and draw its free-body diagram.

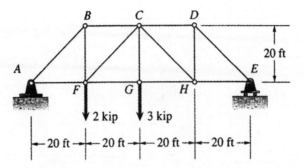

Solution

(a)

1. Imagine the entire truss to be separated or detached from its supports.
2. Use Table 2.1 to determine the number and types of reactions *acting on the truss* at A and E.
3. Draw the free-body diagram of the (detached) truss showing all the external forces *acting on the truss* labeled with their magnitudes and directions. *Assume* the sense of the vectors representing the *reactions acting on the truss*. Include any other relevant information e.g. lengths, angles etc which may help when formulating the equilibrium equations (including the moment equation) for the truss.

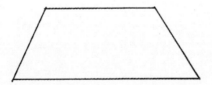

4. Sum moments about point A and write down the moment equilibrium equation.

$$\curvearrowleft + \sum M_A = 0:$$

5. Establish an xy-axes system on the free-body diagram and write down the force equilibrium equations in the x and $y-$ directions:

$$+\rightarrow \sum F_x = 0:$$

$$+\uparrow \ \sum F_y = 0:$$

6. Now solve these equations for the reactions at the supports

(b)

Problem 3.39.

The Howe bridge truss supports loads at F and G.

(a) Draw the free-body diagram of the entire truss and use it to determine the reactions at the supports A and E.

(b) Obtain a section by cutting members CD, CH and GH and draw its free-body diagram.

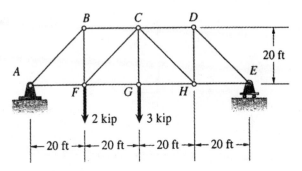

Solution

(a)

1. Imagine the entire truss to be separated or detached from its supports.
2. Use Table 2.1 to determine the number and types of reactions *acting on the truss* at A and E.
3. Draw the free-body diagram of the (detached) truss showing all the external forces *acting on the truss* labeled with their magnitudes and directions. *Assume* the sense of the vectors representing the *reactions acting on the truss*. Include any other relevant information e.g. lengths, angles etc which may help when formulating the equilibrium equations (including the moment equation) for the truss.

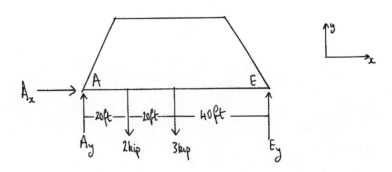

4. Sum moments about point A and write down the moment equilibrium equation.
$$\curvearrowleft + \sum M_A = 0: \quad -2\,(20) - 3\,(40) + 80E_y = 0$$
5. Establish an xy-axes system on the free-body diagram and write down the force equilibrium equations in the x and $y-$ directions:
$$+\rightarrow \sum F_x = 0: \quad A_x = 0.$$
$$+\uparrow \sum F_y = 0: \quad A_y - 2 - 3 + E_y = 0.$$

6. Now solve these equations for the reactions at the supports.

$$A_x = 0, \quad A_y = 3\,kip, \quad E_y = 2\,kip.$$

(b)

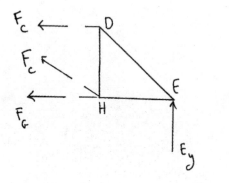

F_c : Magnitude of reaction of C on D, H.

F_G : "   "   "   " G on H

Problem 3.40.

The hydraulic actuator BC exerts a force at C that points along the line from B to C. Treat point A as a pin support. Draw a free body diagram for the arm AD.

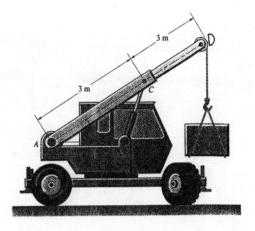

Solution

1. Imagine the arm to be separated or detached from the system.
2. Use Table 2.1 and the information given in the question to determine the number and types of reactions *acting on the arm* at A, C and D.
3. Draw the free-body diagram of the (detached) arm showing all the external forces *acting on the arm* labeled with their magnitudes and directions. *Assume* the sense of the vectors representing the *reactions acting on the arm*. Include any other relevant information e.g. lengths, angles etc which may help when formulating the equilibrium equations (including the moment equation) for the arm.

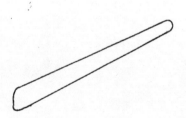

Problem 3.40.

The hydraulic actuator BC exerts a force at C that points along the line from B to C. Treat point A as a pin support. Draw a free body diagram for the arm AD.

Solution

1. Imagine the arm to be separated or detached from the system.
2. Use Table 2.1 and the information given in the question to determine the number and types of reactions *acting on the arm* at A, C and D.
3. Draw the free-body diagram of the (detached) arm showing all the external forces *acting on the arm* labeled with their magnitudes and directions. *Assume* the sense of the vectors representing the *reactions acting on the arm*. Include any other relevant information e.g. lengths, angles etc which may help when formulating the equilibrium equations (including the moment equation) for the arm.

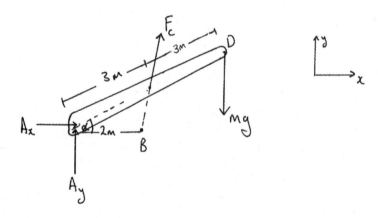

Problem 3.41.

The mass of the crate is m kg. The inclined surface is rough. Draw a free-body diagram of the crate. Explain the significance of each force on the diagram.

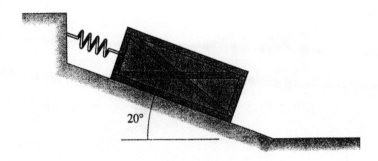

Solution

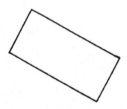

Problem 3.41.

The mass of the crate is m kg. The inclined surface is rough. Draw a free-body diagram of the crate. Explain the significance of each force on the diagram.

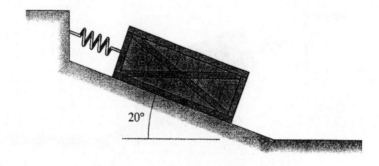

Solution

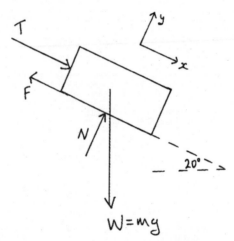

$W = mg$

T: Magnitude of force of spring on crate.
F: " " " " friction " " .
N: " " " normal reaction (from surface) on crate.
W: Crate's weight

Problem 3.42.

The cable AB prevents the 5-Mg (megagram) crate from sliding across the smooth floor of the listing ship's hold. Draw a free-body diagram of the crate explaining the significance of each force on the diagram.

Solution

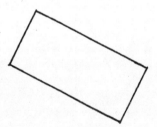

Problem 3.42.

The cable AB prevents the 5-Mg (megagram) crate from sliding across the smooth floor of the listing ship's hold. Draw a free-body diagram of the crate explaining the significance of each force on the diagram.

Solution

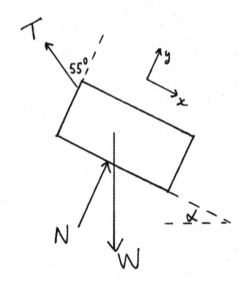

T : Magnitude of force of cable AB on crate.

N :   "   "   reaction from surface on crate.

W : Weight of crate.

Problem 3.43.

The rectangular plate is held in equilibrium by the horizontal force *F. The weight *W acts at the midpoint of the plate. **Draw a** free-body diagram of the plate. Sum moments about the pinned joint A and use this equilibrium equation to show that F **is given** by the equation

$$F = \frac{(b \cos \alpha - h \sin \alpha)}{2(h \cos \alpha + b \sin \alpha)} W.$$

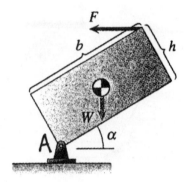

Solution

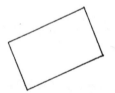

Problem 3.43.

The rectangular plate is held in equilibrium by the horizontal force **F**. The weight **W** acts at the midpoint of the plate. Draw a free-body diagram of the plate. Sum moments about the pinned joint A and use this equilibrium equation to show that F is given by the equation

$$F = \frac{(b \cos\alpha - h \sin\alpha)}{2(h \cos\alpha + b \sin\alpha)} W.$$

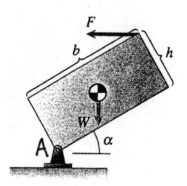

Solution

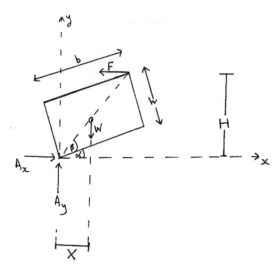

The moment about A of the force with magnitude F is $M_F = HF$, where H is the distance shown in the FBD. In fact, $H = \sqrt{b^2 + h^2} \sin(\alpha + \beta)$, where $\beta = \tan^{-1}\frac{h}{b}$. Similarly, the distance X is given by $X = \left(\frac{1}{2}\right)\sqrt{b^2 + h^2}\cos(\alpha + \beta)$ (remember that the weight **W** acts at the midpoint of the plate). The sum of the moments about A is then:

$$\curvearrowleft + \sum M_A = 0: \quad F\sqrt{b^2 + h^2}\sin(\alpha + \beta) - \left(\frac{W}{2}\right)\sqrt{b^2 + h^2}\cos(\alpha + \beta) = 0$$

Noting that $\cos\beta = \dfrac{b}{\sqrt{b^2 + h^2}}$, and $\sin\beta = \dfrac{h}{\sqrt{b^2 + h^2}}$, the moment equation reduces to (upon application of double angle formulas)

$$F(b \sin\alpha + h \cos\alpha) - \left(\frac{W}{2}\right)(b \cos\alpha - h \sin\alpha) = 0,$$

from which we obtain

$$F = \frac{(b \cos\alpha - h \sin\alpha)}{2(h \cos\alpha + b \sin\alpha)} W.$$

Problem 3.44.

The forklift is stationary. The front wheels are free to turn but the rear wheels are locked. W_L and W_F represent the weights of the load and the truck + operator, respectively. Draw a free-body diagram of the forklift. Be sure to label all the force magnitudes and directions explaining the significance of each force on the diagram.

Solution

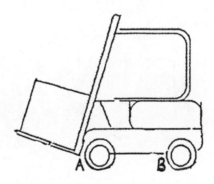

Problem 3.44.

The forklift is stationary. The front wheels are free to turn but the rear wheels are locked. W_L and W_F represent the weights of **the load and the truck + operator, respectively. Draw a free-body diagram of the forklift. Be sure to label all the force magnitudes and directions** explaining the significance of each force on the diagram.

Solution

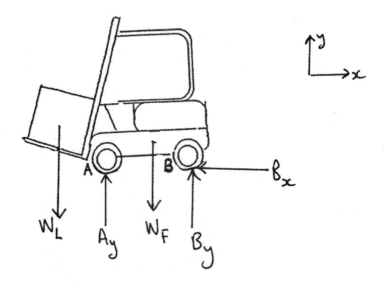

A_y : Magnitude of surface reaction at A on forklift.

B_x, B_y : Magnitudes of surface reaction at B on forklift (contact with a rough surface — see Table 2·1)

Problem 3.45.

Draw a free-body diagram for the linkage ABC. Be sure to label all the force magnitudes and directions explaining the significance of each force on the diagram. The collar at A is smooth. Neglect the weight of each bar.

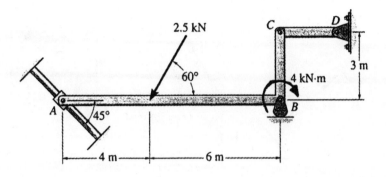

Solution

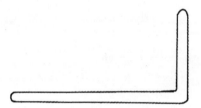

Problem 3.45.

Draw a free-body diagram for the linkage ABC. Be sure to label all the force magnitudes and directions explaining the significance of each force on the diagram. The collar at A is smooth. Neglect the weight of each bar.

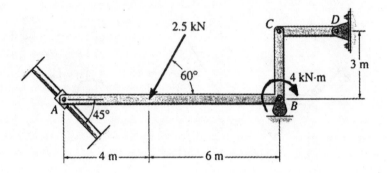

Solution

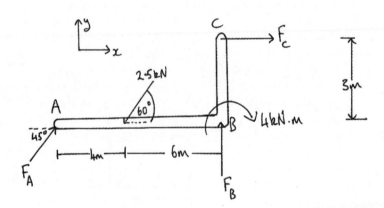

F_A, F_B, F_C : Magnitude of reactions from supports A, B and C on bar linkage.

Problem 3.46.

By drawing a free-body diagram of the beam, determine the reactions on the beam at A and B. Neglect the weight of the beam.

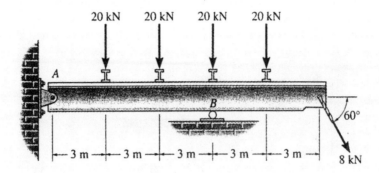

Solution

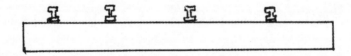

Problem 3.46.

By drawing a free-body diagram of the beam, determine the reactions on the beam at A and B. Neglect the weight of the beam.

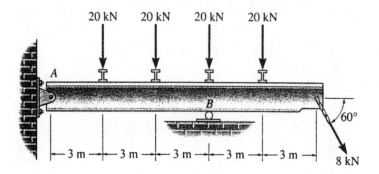

Solution

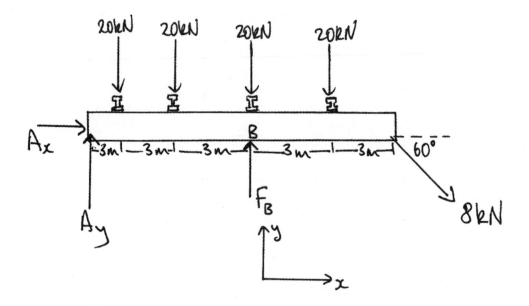

1. Sum moments about point A and write down the moment equilibrium equation.

$$\curvearrowright + \sum M_A = 0: \quad -20\,(3) - 20\,(6) - 20(9) - 20\,(12) - 8\sin 60°\,(15) + F_B\,(9) = 0$$

Consequently, $F_B = 78.2$ kN.

2. Establish an xy-axes system on the free-body diagram and write down the force equilibrium equations in the x and $y-$ directions:

$$+\rightarrow \sum F_x = 0: \quad A_x + 8\cos 60° = 0.$$

Hence, $A_x = -4 \ kN$.

$$+\uparrow \sum F_y = 0: \quad -20 - 20 - 20 - 20 - 8\sin 60° + 78.2 + A_y = 0.$$

Hence $A_y = 8.71$ kN.

Problem 3.47.

The shelf supports the electric motor which has a mass m_m kg and mass center at G_m. The platform upon which it rests has a mass of m_P kg and mass center at G_P. Assuming that the single bolt B holds the shelf up and the bracket bears against the smooth wall at A, draw a free-body diagram of the shelf.

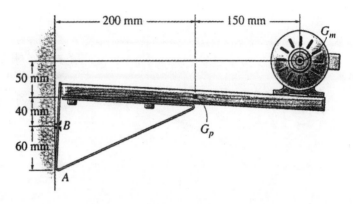

Solution

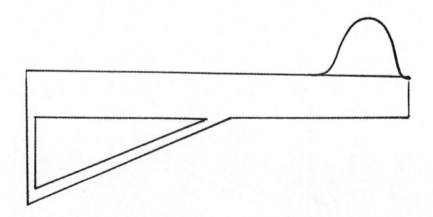

Problem 3.47.

The shelf supports the electric motor which has a mass m_m kg and mass center at G_m. The platform upon which it rests has a mass of m_P kg and mass center at G_P. Assuming that the single bolt B holds the shelf up and the bracket bears against the smooth wall at A, draw a free-body diagram of the shelf.

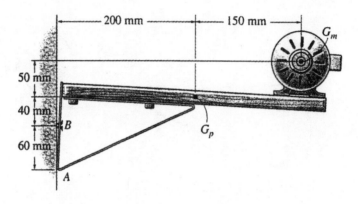

Solution

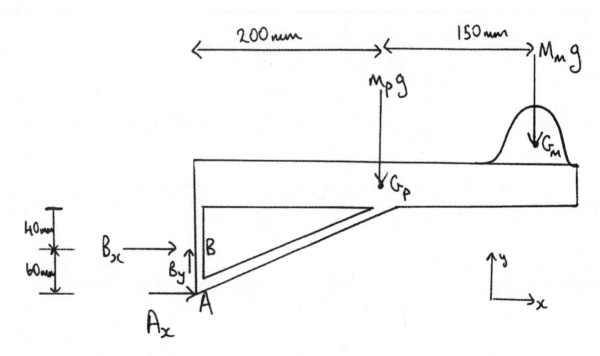

Problem 3.48.

The platform assembly has a weight of $*W_P$ and a center of gravity at G_1. It is intended to support a maximum load of M_{max} lb placed at point G_2. Use a free-body diagram of the assembly to write down the moment equilibrium equation about point D. Deduce the value of the smallest counterweight W_B that should be placed at B in order to prevent the platform from tipping over.

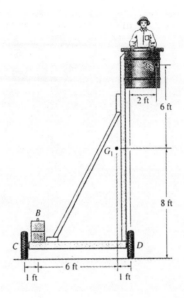

Solution

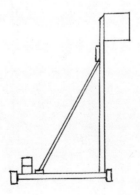

Problem 3.48.

The platform assembly has a weight of $*\mathbf{W_P}$ and center of gravity at G_1. It is intended to support a maximum load of M_{max} lb placed at point G_2. Use a free-body diagram of the assembly to write down the moment equilibrium equation about point D. Deduce the value of the smallest counterweight W_B that should be placed at B in order to prevent the platform from tipping over.

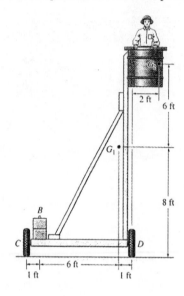

Solution

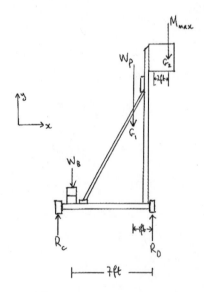

When tipping occurs, $R_C = 0$:

$$\curvearrowleft + \sum M_D = 0: \quad -M_{max}\,(2) + W_P\,(1) + W_B\,(7) = 0$$

$$W_B = \frac{2M_{max} - W_P}{7} \text{ lb.}$$

Problem 3.49.

The mass of the trailer is M_T megagrams. The truck is stationary and the wheels of the trailer can turn freely (the road exerts no horizontal force on the wheels). The hitch at B can be modeled as a pin support. Draw the free-body diagram of the trailer.

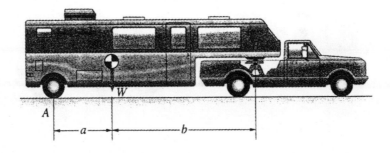

Solution

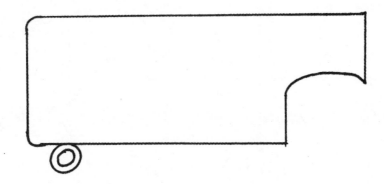

Problem 3.49.

The mass of the trailer is M_T megagrams. The truck is stationary and the wheels of the trailer can turn freely (the road exerts no horizontal force on the wheels). The hitch at B can be modeled as a pin support. Draw the free-body diagram of the trailer.

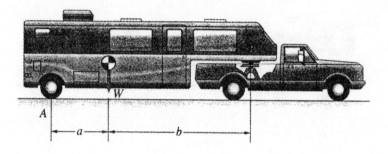

Solution

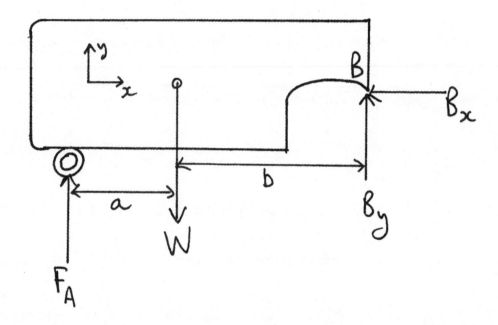

Problem 3.50.

The force has known magnitude F and the couple has known magnitude M. Use a free-body diagram of the assembly to show that the reaction at A has magnitude $\dfrac{LF - M}{L}$.

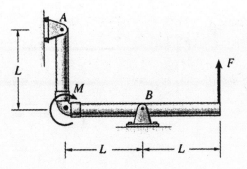

Solution

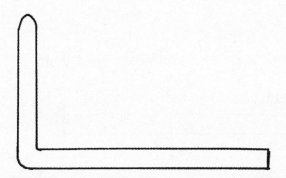

Problem 3.50.

The force has known magnitude F and the couple has known magnitude M. Use a free-body diagram of the assembly to show that the reaction at A has magnitude $\dfrac{LF - M}{L}$.

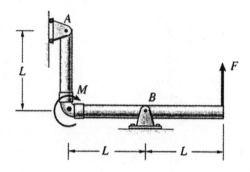

Solution

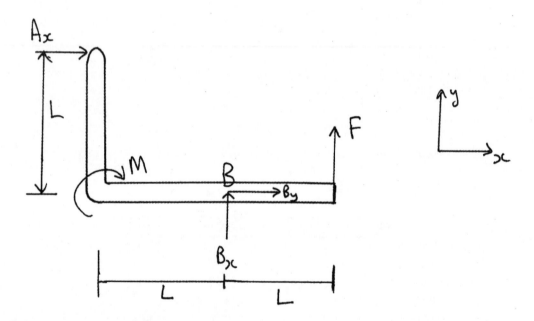

$$\curvearrowleft + \sum M_B = 0: \quad -LA_x + LF - M = 0$$

$$A_x = \frac{LF - M}{L}.$$

Appendix

Questions to Accompany Working Model Simulations—Statics

This CD is designed to give you a better understanding of many problems and examples in your text through simulation. Using the powerful Working Model™ engine, we have turned 25 problems and examples from this book into educational simulations. These simulations help you:

- Visualize the forces working in an example or problem and see their effects
- See forces and vectors change over time
- View and analyze results of the example both numerically and graphically Change preset values, and learn how these factors affect the example and its outcome
- Alter the example using the features of Working Model Answer questions that test and extend your understanding of the textual material
- All materials were designed for ease of use. The CD is self-installing and contains all the software needed on this CD. If you have questions about installation, please consult the README file located on the CD.

This appendix contains questions to accompany each simulation. These questions first test your understanding of the simulation, and then try and challenge you to learn more.

3.1

∗ Consider extreme cases with the springs and masses at their maximum and/or minimum values.

1. Is the total displacement of mass B as measured from the support different in the following two cases:

Case 1: A is maximum and B is minimum

Case 2: B is maximum and A is minimum

2. Explain the differences observed in the above comparison.

3. Does the value of the spring constant make any difference in the above comparison?

3.2

∗ To the student—you may have to hit the RUN button repeatedly to allow this simulation to settle down to rest.

1. What combination of masses and spring constants will cause the collar A to come to rest highest on the bar?

2. What combination of masses and spring constants will cause the collar A to come to rest lowest on the bar?

3. Given that the mass B is 5 kg, find the range of values for h which can be obtained by changing the spring constant and the mass A .

4. Given that the mass A is 10 kg, find the range of values for h which can be obtained by changing the spring constant and the mass B .

3.3

1. If mass A is 1 kg, what must mass B be for equilibrium?
2. If mass B is 50 kg, what must mass A be for equilibrium?
3. If mass A is 50 kg, what must mass B be for equilibrium.
4. If mass B is 1 kg, what must mass A be for equilibrium?

3.4

1. What combination of buoyancy and drag result in the smallest angle "alpha"?
2. What combination of buoyancy and drag result in the largest angle "alpha"?
3. What combination or cominations of buoyancy and drag result in an angle "alpha;; of 20 degrees? If there are multiple combinations, find three examples.

3.5

1. For offset $h = 0$ and offset b allowed to very, describe the position of point A relative to the two pulleys.
2. With offsets $h = 2$ and $b = 5$, find the angle between the two cords at A.
3. With offsets $h = 2$ and $b = 4$, find the angle between the two cords at A.

5.1

1. Is it possible to set the problem up so that the bar from which A is suspended remains horizontal while the bar from which C and D hang rotates clockwise? Describe how to accomplish this.
2. Is it possible to set the problem up so that the bar from which A is suspended remains horizontal while the bar from which C and D hang rotates counterclockwise? Describe how to accomplish this.

5.2

1. Is it possible to load the forklift so that the reaction at B is zero? If so, find the load necessary to accomplish this. What does this situation imply about the safety of the forklift and operator?
2. What happens if we load the forklift with a load larger than that found in the question above? Is there a safety problem in this situation?
3. Is it possible to load the forklift so that the reaction at B is larger than the reaction at A? Place the load at the a distance "a" from the front wheel A.
4. Consider tying a helium balloon at a point a distance "a" from the front wheel. How much "lift" would this balloon need to produce to make reactions at A and B equal?

5.3

1. Using the strongest possible spring and the lightest possible rod as defined by the sliders in the model, find the equilibrium angle.
2. Using the strongest possible spring and the heaviest possible rod as defined by the sliders in the model, find the equilibrium angle.
3. Using the weakest possible spring and the lightest possible rod as defined by the sliders in the model, find the equilibrium angle.
4. Using the weakest possible spring and the heaviest possible rod as defined by the sliders in the model, find the equilibrium angle.

5.4

* This model moves through a series of static configurations—Let it cycle through until it has generated plots with the length of the hydraulic cylinder ranging from less than 1.6 m to more than 3.2 m. Then use the slider at the bottom left to step through the recorded sequence one step at a time. Neglect the starting transient plot segment.

1. Find the x and y which correspond to the largest value of force in the hydraulic cylinder.
2. Find the x and y which correspond to the smallest value of force in the hydraulic cylinder.
3. Find the x and y which correspond to a force of 40 kN in the hydraulic cylinder.
4. Find the force in the hydraulic cylinder which corresponds to an x coordinate of 1.00 meters.

5.5

1. Use the model to generate numbers for a plot of Tension in Actuator vs Length of Actuator. Is the plot monotonic?
2. Use your plot to determine the actuator length where the tension in the actuator is 800 lbs. Set the model to this length (as closely as possible) and verify your answer.
3. Use your plot to determine the tension in the actuator where the length of the actuator is 30 in. Set the model to this length (as closely as possible) and verify your answer.

6.1

1. Why is there no force in member BC?
2. Would there be a force in BC if we moved the vertical force at D to C?
3. Would there be a force in BD if we moved the vertical force at D to C?
4. What would happen if we allowed the force at D to be directed upward?

6.2

* We need to show the forces at B on Member $ABCD$ and at E on member CEG

1. What Weights W produce the largest and smallest tensions in BE?
2. How is the tension in the horizontal section of the rope related to the Weight, W?
3. Assume that we weld the pulley to CEG at G, glued the rope permanently to the pulley, and removed the section of rope parallel to CEG. —Would the forces acting on CEG, $ABCD$, and/or BE change?

6.3

1. What is the mechanical advantage, (the force at C divided by the force at the handle) when the force at A is largest?
2. What is the mechanical advantage, (the force at C divided by the force at the handle) when the force at A is only 7.5 lb?
3. How large a load could you apply with your hands to such a tool? Write a paragraph explaining how you would apply such a load.
4. How large a force at C could you apply if you were able to stabilize the bottom handle in a deep groove and stand on the top part of the handle, exerting all of your weight on the handle?

6.4

1. Set the force at E to -8.00 N. At what value of the force at C do the axial forces in AC and DG have approximately the same magnitude?
2. Assume a total loading of 12 N (the sum of the loads at C and E). Which combination of loads (in the ranges provided by the sliders) gives the largest load magnitude in member BE?
3. Assume a total loading of 12 N (the sum of the loads at C and E). Which combination of loads (in the ranges provided by the sliders) gives the smallest load magnitude in member BE?

4. Assume a total loading of 14 N (the sum of the loads at C and E). Which combination of loads (in the ranges provided by the sliders) gives the largest load magnitude in any member in the truss? In which member does this load occur and what is the magnitude of the load?

6.5

1. Plot the equilibrium angle versus the spring constant over the entire range of spring constants available through the slider.

2. Use the plot to predict the equilibrium angle for spring constants of 1000, 2000, and 3000 N/m.

3. Use the relationship given to to find the spring constant which will give an equilibrium angle of 20 degrees for an applied force of −2000 N.

4. Use the relationship given to to find the applied force which will give an equilibrium angle of 20 degrees for a spring constant of 1500 N/m.

6.6

∗ This model moves through a series of static configurations— First, set the load W to the desired value and press the RUN button. Let it cycle through until it has generated plota plot across the span of the graph provided. Then use the slider at the bottom left to step through the recorded sequence one step at a time. Neglect the starting transient plot segment.

1. For $W = 300$ lb, find the height h corresponding to a force in the actuator of 768 lb.

2. For $W = 300$ lb, find the height h corresponding to a force in the actuator of 640 lb.

3. For $W = 200$ lb, find the height h corresponding to a force in the actuator of 512 lb.

4. For $W = 120$ lb, find the height h corresponding to a force in the actuator of 300 lb.

7.1

1. What is the largest force per unit length that can be accommodated if there is a magnitude limit of 20,000 N at A?

2. What is the largest force per unit length that can be accommodated if there is a magnitude limit of 17,000 N at C?

3. What is the largest force per unit length that can be accommodated if there is a magnitude limit of 2,500 N at B?

4. If all three limits above are applied at the same time, what is the largest force per unit length that can be accommodated by the frame? What are the corresponding load magnitudes at A, B, and C, and which of these actually reaches its limit at the maximum loading?

7.2

1. Find the range of values for the reaction at B when the hole is moved from one extreme position to the other.

2. For what value of the horizontal coordinate of the hole's center is the reaction at B equal to 200 N? Interpolate to get a closer value than the simulation provides.

3. Find the range of values for the reaction at A when the hole is moved from one extreme position to the other.

4. For what value of the horizontal coordinate of the hole's center is the reaction at A equal to 290 N? Interpolate to get a closer value than the simulation provides.

9.1

1. Set the left mass to 45 kg and the right mass to 30 kg. At what angle of the left incline does the system slip?

2. Set the left mass to 30 kg and the right mass to 30 kg. At what angle of the left incline does the system slip?

3. Set the left mass to 45 kg and the right mass to 45 kg. At what angle of the left incline does the system slip? Is this the same angle as in the previous question? If they are not the same, what is the difference?

4. Set the left mass to 30 kg and the right mass to 50 kg. At what angle of the left incline does the system slip?

5. Create a mathematical model for this system and verify it by using values that can be verified using the simulation. Then use it to find the angle of the left incline at which slipping occurs for a left mass of 35 kg and a right mass of 60 kg.

9.2

1. Use analysis to develop a plot of angle of ladder at slip vs coefficient of friction for coefficents between 0.1 and 1.0. Draw the plot. Predict the coefficient of friction at which slip will occur for the situation in the simulation and verify it using the simulation.

2. Use your analysis to determine how high up the ladder the man could go before it slipped if the coefficient of friction is 0.45.

9.3

∗ The units are NOT metric in this one. Change the units onthe sliders. The problem statement has correct units.

1. For a 3000 lb airplane and a coefficient of friction of 1.00, find the maximum trust that can be developed before the aircraft begins to move. (Set the mass and friction and the slowly increase the thrust by moving the Thrust Force slider.)

2. For a 2000 lb airplane and a coefficient of friction of 1.00, find the maximum trust that can be developed before the aircraft begins to move. (Set the mass and friction and the slowly increase the thrust by moving the Thrust Force slider.)

3. For a thrust level of 1000 lb, and a 3000 lb aircraft, find the minimum coefficient of friction that will keep the aircraft from beginning to slip.

4. For a thrust level of 1000 lb, and a coefficient of friction of 0.8, find the minimum weight aircraft,that will not slip.

9.4

1. Can you create a situation in which the refrigerator tips without slipping? If so, describe how you did it. Back your description up with analysis. Show what happens with the simulation.

2. Can you create a situation in which the refrigerator slips without tipping? If so, describe how you did it. Back your description up with analysis. Show what happens with the simulation.

3. Can you create a situation in which the refrigerator slips and tips simultaneously? If so, describe how you did it. Back your description up with analysis. Show what happens with the simulation.

9.5

∗ The force on *A* is the wrong way to move *C* upward. It moves *A* upward!!! We need to reverse its direction and move *C* upward. As it is, *A* flies away and *B* and *C* sit there and do nothing!!!!!

The following question will work once the simulation is fixed.

1. Find the minimum force necessary to inititate slipping using the simulation. Set up an analysis of the problem and verify your findings.

I can think of no other questions for this simulation.